The Story of Canada Blackie

Anne P. L. Field

SING SING PRISONERS WEEP
AT CANADA BLACKIE'S BIER

Warden Osborne Almost in Tears as He Pronounces
Eulogy of Convict Who Made Good in Aiding
Mutual Welfare League

HEATHEN EDITIONS
THEIR BOOKS. OUR WAY.

Published in the good ole United States of America
by Heathen Editions, an imprint of
Heathen Creative
P.O. Box 588
Point Pleasant, WV 25550-0588

Heathen Editions are available at quantity discounts.
For information and more tomfoolery, check us out online:

heatheneditions.com

@heatheneditions
#heathenedition

First published 1915
Heathen Edition published March 30, 2023

Book and cover design by Sheridan Cleland
Set in 11pt Plantin Std
Chapters in Special Elite

ISBN: 978-1-948316-29-3

FIRST HEATHEN EDITION

To
BLACKIE'S PALS
This little book is
gratefully and affectionately
dedicated

POLICEMAN MURDERED

By Three Burglars in Cobleskill This Morning—Assassins Escaped.

(Special Dispatch.)

Binghamton, Nov. 27.—Night Policeman Wilson of Cobleskill was shot and killed by three burglars in Cobleskill early this morning. The assassins escaped.

FOUR BULLET WOUNDS.

Cobleskill, N. Y., Nov. 27.—Night Watchman Matthew Wilson was found lying dead upon the steps of Martin B. Borst's grocery store at 2 o'clock this morning with four bullet wounds in his body. An investigation of the premises revealed a number of burglar's tools lying in the rear of the store. Beside the dead man's body was his revolver with five chambers empty. Four shots which had probably been fired by the watchman, had penetrated the plate glass windows in the stores opposite. Five men were seen running in the direction of the railroad tracks. They managed to escape in the darkness but several searching parties are scouring the country hereabouts. It is thought that the men were in the act of robbing the store when surprised by the watchman, who attacked them with the above result.

NIGHT WATCHMAN DIED ON DUTY.

Burglars Emptied Their Weapons Into Body of Their Disturber.

Cobleskill, Nov. 27.—Night Watchman Matthew Wilson was found dead upon the steps of a grocery store at 2 o'clock this morning, with four bullet wounds in his body. An investigation of the premises revealed a number of burglar's tool lying in the rear of the store. Beside the dead man's body was his revolver, with five chambers empty. Four shots which had probably been fired by the watchman, had penetrated windows in the stores opposite.

Five men were seen running in the direction of the railroad tracks. They managed to escape in the darkness. They were surprised by the night watchman, who attacked them.

BURGLARS KILL A WATCHMAN.

Victim Found Dead in the Street in Cobleskill—Murderers Escape.

COBLESKILL, N. Y., Nov. 27.—Matthew Wilson, night watchman in this village, was shot and instantly killed just before 2 o'clock this morning by a supposed gang of burglars. Four men were seen coming down West Main Street just preceding the shooting, and it is supposed Wilson came in contact with them at the corner of Main and Union Streets, and was then shot down. Many shots were fired, the watchman's revolver being emptied, and plate glass windows across the street were shattered by shots evidently fired by the burglars.

The fusillade aroused the people, and the night watchman was found lying face downward in front of M. D. Borst's store, dead, with four bullet holes in his body. The toolhouse of the Delaware and Hudson River Railroad Company had been broken open and a quantity of tools taken. They were found near the scene of the murder.

The village authorities have offered a reward of $500 for the arrest and conviction of the murderers, and a large number of men are making a search of the near-by woods and uninhabited buildings in quest of the men.

LAST OF "YEGG" GANG.

Canada Blackie to be Tried for Murder of Cobleskill Bank Watchman.

Cobleskill, N. Y., Feb. 7.—John Murphy, alias "Canada" Blackie, alias "John Hamilton," was brought from the Erie county penitentiary, Buffalo, to the Schoharie county jail to-day. This completes the arrests of the living members of the "Yegg" gang, accused of the murder of Matthew Wilson, night watchman of the First National Bank of Cobleskill on November 26th, 1900.

The gang consisted of James Sullivan, alias "Whitney" Sullivan, who was convicted and sentenced to be electrocuted the week beginning December 8, 1901; William O'Connor, alias "William Montgomery," alias "James Sullivan," alias "William Hinch," alias "Goat" Hinch, who was convicted at the January court and sentenced to be electrocuted, week beginning March 3, 1902; Edward Jackson, alias "Dublin," who pleaded guilty to burglary and was sentenced for ten years; William Harris, alias "Sheeny" Harris, who turned state's evidence and is now awaiting trial at Schoharie and Charles Foulke, alias "Ballard," who was killed in Virginia by the explosion of nitro-glycerine.

Canada Blackie will be tried at the April term of the court at Schoharie.

Programme

Heathenry:
Overture

Overture? We'll explain in a moment, but first: what began as
a simple, straightforward Heathen Edition slowly turned into
a research rabbit hole whose accumulation of details began
to paint a more tragic picture the deeper we went.

To read Anne P. L. Field's *The Story of Canada Blackie*,
by itself, is to be left wanting more because it's heavy on
letters penned by Blackie and light on actual biographical
sustenance — we still don't know what the E in John E.
Murphy stands for! She alludes far more than she elaborates,
and she commits *the* sin that so many prison reform writers
of the early 20th century sought to avoid like the plague: she
makes it sentimental. However, she was first a poet, practic-
ing in a medium whose primary tenet is less is more, and she
bore such a striking resemblance to Blackie's own mother
that he, once the courage was summoned, asked if he could
refer to her as such, so we believe her sentimentalism can
and should be forgiven because what poet-mother wouldn't
be sentimental (all jokes aside) when crafting a biography of
her son (or "son") after he's unnecessarily succumbed (rela-
tively young) to a disease unnecessarily acquired in a wholly

irresponsible system that (suspiciously) had him pegged all wrong from the start?

Truly, once Blackie's whole, tragic story is realized — as much as can now be gleaned from its many pieces and disparate sources — it's so infuriating that all you can do is ball your hands into fists and curse.

Was he innocent? Of crime in general, no — he never denied being a criminal — but of the crime that netted him life behind bars he was likely innocent. But we're getting ahead of ourselves.

J.B. Kerfoot in his review of Field's book for *Life* stated, "while it is sentimentally told, it is manifestly and significantly true."[1] And we agree one hundred percent, yet Field's book, on its own, lacks the depth we crave, which is why we have fleshed it out with as much Blackie information as we could amass. Which isn't to say that you should skip over Mrs. Field's book entirely as it's a crucial piece of the puzzle.

So, why an overture?

Because in amassing all of the additional bits and pieces that we've collected for this edition, a lot of repetition and overlap — a musicality, if you will — presents itself as each author recounts many of the same anecdotes, but from naturally varied points of view. For example, after meeting Donald Lowrie for the first time, Blackie wrote him a letter which manifests as near pseudo-chorus in our edition since Lowrie published a portion in his book *My Life Out of Prison*, Mrs. Field reprinted a portion in her book, and still yet Osborne reprinted a portion in his *Society and Prisons*. Yet, each author presents their version with such subtle variations that a quasi-*Rashomon* effect materializes in its repetition.

That is both a warning and a directive — there is quite a bit of repetition in this edition but *pay attention* — because the *why* of Canada Blackie is a puzzle of details easily overlooked. To illustrate: an early review of the book by *The*

---

[1] Kerfoot, J.B. (1915, September 23). The Latest Books. *Life*, 66(1717), p.568.

New York Times Book Review is the **only** place we've found a not inconsequential piece of the puzzle: "It was at Dannemora that a guard tore to shreds before his eyes the only photograph that Blackie had of his own mother."[2]

Fists yet?

In keeping with musicality, we have labeled the table of contents "programme" and structured our edition in such a way as to thread you through the narrative as lyrically as possible, which is mostly in chronological order — more so in order of original publication, but not always.

Briefly, we begin with [spoilers ahead] the original introduction by Thomas Mott Osborne, then Anne's poem "Banked Fires," which didn't appear in the first edition of *The Story of Canada Blackie*, but may have been added to a later edition since the poem was published after the book. The book arrived August 6, 1915,[3] while the poem followed in *The Survey* of December 4th,[4] and the text preceding the poem is taken from a version that was syndicated in newspapers soon after.[5]

We believe experiencing her poem before her narrative better underpins the point that she was a poet first, a good one, and the lyricism of the former, in part, explains the sentimentalism of the latter.

Next is an excerpt from Donald Lowrie's second book *My Life Out of Prison*, which emerged in book form after newspaper serialization sometime during the week of March 28–April 3, 1915.[6] In it, we meet No. 32,378 in solitary at Auburn, and for reasons unknown Lowrie never refers to him as "Canada Blackie," only John E. Murphy, or Jack

---

[2] Canada Blackie's Story of Prison Life. (1915, August 29). *The New York Times Book Review*, p. 307.

[3] Prison Reform? How? When? Why? (1915, August 1). *The New York Times Book Review*, p. 274.

[4] "Banked Fires." (1915, December 4) *The Survey*, 35(10), pp. 234–235.

[5] In keeping with repetition, we have included most of this same information in another footnote later.

[6] (1915, April 4) Latest Publications: Books Received During the Week Ended March 31. *The New York Times Book Review*, p. 124.

ch. ends p. xiv

for short, however that works. There's no sentimentality in
Lowrie's writing (you'll know what we mean soon enough),
and it provides a good counterbalance to Field's sympathies.

Next, we must include a mention of Thomas Mott
Osborne's first prison reform book, and an explanation for
its exclusion. Osborne read Lowrie's first book *My Life in
Prison* soon after it was serialized from August–December
1911 and published June1912 and was so inspired he will-
ingly entered Auburn Prison as an inmate for one week in
September–October 1913, then published the book *Within
Prison Walls* about that experience on Tuesday, May 26,
1914.[7] In it, Osborne details his daily interactions with a
Jack/John Murphy, but it's not the same John E. Murphy,
No. 32,378, of this book, instead being Auburn No. 32,177.
However, it's a book very much worth reading, if you're
interested,[8] because that week of Osborne's dialogues with
the other Murphy is what birthed the now legendary Mutual
Welfare League.

Then there is Mrs. Field's book whose strongest element,
all previous criticisms aside, is the many letters penned by
Blackie as those are the closest we get to an autobiography,
and they reveal that Blackie had a deep soul not many of his
contemporaries had the opportunity to experience.

That is followed by an excerpt from Osborne's book *Society and Prisons*, published Tuesday, July 18, 1916,[9] in
which Osborne gives a great biographical sketch of Murphy,
now referring to him as Canada Blackie, and details Blackie's liberation from solitary through to his eventual pardon.
Again, there is repetition, but Osborne supplies certain
details that Mrs. Field doesn't.

Then, in case you thought this was all suddenly getting
far too sentimental, Lowrie returns with three chapters from

---

[7] New Books Published. (1914, May 28). *The Hartford Daily Courant*. p. A8.

[8] If our edition hasn't been published by the time you read this, it will be soon!

[9] The Latest Books. (1916, July 21). *The Brooklyn Daily Times*. p. A5.

his final book *Back in Prison—Why?*,[10] which broadcasts the strongest *Rashomon* effect, yet, in his matter-of-fact delivery of how it was decided when and who should give Blackie his pardon. Again, details.

Four articles follow: three from the *New-York Tribune* with Lewis Wood's "Leader Among Criminals the Wreck of a Genius" offering one surprising detail we can't find anywhere else, and one from *The Kingston Daily Freeman* which gives us probably the best account of the first time Blackie laid eyes on Anne.

Then, wrapping up, we give Osborne final say with a speech he delivered to the Republican Club of New York City, wherein he again sketches Blackie's bio before reminding us: just say no![11]

And if this is an Overture, then there should naturally follow a Coda, and Osborne's summation and final recap of Blackie's life, we believe, is a good lead-in because you're going to have some questions and that's what we intend to accomplish with our Coda: to answer as many questions as possible with details we've been able to extract from myriad newspapers but in articles far too short to warrant chapters of their own like the articles mentioned above.

For example, we spoil nothing by repeating that this entire story exists only because night watchman Matthew Wilson was shot and killed in Cobleskill, New York, on the morning of November 27, 1900. His lifeless body was discovered at 2 A.M. on the steps of Martin B. Borst's grocery with four bullet holes in it. Five men were seen fleeing the scene and stolen "burglar's tools" were discovered nearby.[12]

In alleged connection to the murder, John E. Murphy, alias "Canada Blackie," alias "John Hamilton," was identified

---

[10] It's first time in print since it was originally serialized in 1925! A proper Heathen Edition of the entire book will be published shortly.

[11] The Story of "Canada Blackie." (1915, May 22). *The Christian Work*, 98(2516), pp. 663-64.

[12] Policeman Murdered: By Three Burglars in Cobleskill This Morning—Assassins Escaped. (1900, November 27). *Elmira Gazette*. p. A1.

ch. ends next p.

as the leader and last-to-be-arrested member of the "Yegg" Gang, whose also-indicted members consisted:

- James Sullivan, alias Whitey Sullivan, who was convicted and sentenced to be electrocuted the week beginning December 8, 1901.
- William O'Connor, alias William Montgomery, alias William Hinch, alias Goat Hinch, who was convicted in January 1902 and sentenced to be electrocuted the week beginning March 3.
- Edward Jackson, alias Dublin Ned, who pled guilty to burglary and was sentenced to ten years.
- William Harris, alias Sheeny Harris, who turned state's evidence.
- Charles Foulke, alias Ballard, who was killed in Virginia by "the explosion of nitro-glycerine."[13]

Keep an eye out: "Sheeny" might be "shady."

Finally, regarding the text of this edition, we've updated some words to reflect their modern equivalents (good-night is now goodnight; to-day is now today, etc.), and we've appended over 100 footnotes to enhance your reading and identify our source materials where appropriate.

Additionally, most sections begin with facsimiles of the original sources, which we believe lends further authenticity to this *insane* true story.

With that, the stage is set, and we begin——

---

[13] Last of 'Yegg' Gang: Canada Blackie to be Tried for Murder of Cobleskill Bank Watchman. (1902, February 8). *Democrat Chronicle*. p. A1.

Introduction

Deep down in the heart of every man is an innate love of humanity — a spark of that divine love that redeems the world — the spirit of God.

The old prison system with its repression of all natural instincts — its silence, its espionage, its brutality — tended to crush and deform the character of every man who came under its control — officers and prisoners alike. It is a proof of the divine nature of man that in spite of all the torture that stupidity could inflict, the soul of the prisoner would not be crushed. It could be driven into revolt, but it could not be killed.

So we find in the prisons a passionate friendship for down-trodden humanity — a loyalty, a splendid spirit of cooperation, a vigorous endurance which, if it could be utilized by society, would tend to uplift the whole community.

Can it be so utilized?

The story of Canada Blackie gives the answer.

In his case a powerful destructive force was turned and made constructive. The man who was regarded as the most dangerous criminal in the State, became, through the same strength that made him dangerous, a loyal and trusted friend of the authorities — helping to build up a new and better prison system by the sympathetic help of the prisoners themselves.

The old prison system had seriously crippled him; but wasted by disease he was yet able to do a man's part in the brief time allotted to him; and by the force of a great example to help make firm the foundations of a new penology.

For many years to come, the name of Canada Blackie will be an inspiration to all who knew him, both within and without the prison.

Thomas Mott Osborne,[1]
Warden of Sing Sing Prison.
July 7, 1915.

---

[1] Thomas Mott Osborne (1859–1926) was an American prison administrator, prison reformer, industrialist, and New York State political reformer. In 1912, he was inspired to read *My Life In Prison* by Donald Lowrie, a former inmate of San Quentin prison in California, which he pinpointed as the genesis of his prison reform crusade. The following year he was appointed chairman of a new State Commission on Prison Reform, then spent six days of imprisonment as "Tom Brown" in Auburn Prison. He recorded his experiences in his 1914 book *Within Prison Walls*, whose publication made him the most prominent prison reform crusader of his day. The following year he was appointed warden of Sing Sing.

Banked Fires

The whole country is following the fight against Thomas Mott Osborne and the things he stands for at Sing Sing. These verses have been hailed as one of the most powerful interpretations yet made of the man and his method of dealing with other men.

The verses themselves have an interesting history. Osborne, millionaire, former mayor of Auburn, and a member of the board of Auburn prison, startled the country a couple years ago by donning prison garb, going through the mill at Auburn prison to see what it was like, and starting a revolution in methods of handling the prisoners there. One of the prisoners the guards feared most, keeping him shut up in a cell, was Canada Blackie, burglar and peterman.[1] Osborne talked with him, trusted him, treated him as a man, and the story of his changed life is one of the most remarkable personal transformations in all prison history. It is told in the book bearing Canada Blackie's name, written by Mrs. Field, the author of these verses.

Mrs. Field was a guest of Mr. Osborne at Auburn when

[1] Safecracker.

Canada Blackie saw her and was overcome by her resemblance to his mother. When Mr. Osborne was made warden of Sing Sing, Canada Blackie was transferred there, and when he died last March forty-eight of his fellow prisoners sent Mrs. Field a pendant in the form of a "gold heart," the nickname Canada Blackie had had for his mother, in appreciation of the care and nursing Mrs. Field had given him unstintedly in the last year of his life! One man put into it his savings for three years, and the only instructions to the jeweler were to make it with as little alloy as possible.

Mrs. Field was inspired to write the poem "Banked Fires" by the recent bitter attacks on the warden of Sing Sing.

Of prisoners and prisons I had talked
To eager listeners that afternoon,
And then at twilight through the pines I walked
To a poet's cabin, where a young white moon
Swung in the treetops, and a silver star
Silently pointed to the door ajar.

Solace I needed, for my seething mind
Ached with its effort. Had I caused the blind
To see? Did the deaf ears hear?
Ah, how I longed to make my message clear!

Then the poet came and drew me in
To a great room half-swathed in shadows, where
He bade me rest within a well-worn chair
Before the hearth — which seemed quite cold and gray
To me — but suddenly I saw my host begin
To stir the ashes in his gentle way,
And soon he found a spark, and then a flame
Leaped upward leading others, till the room
Became a thing of light! The gloom
Had gone and nothing was the same.

Then the poet smiled and glanced at me—
"I seek for hidden sparks, you see,
Within the ashes, for I bank my fire
That it may spring to life at my desire.
But tell me why this radiance on your face?
Do you behold a vision? Has my spark
Kindled a flaming thought?"

                    Swiftly I turned[2]
To answer. God in His grace
Has spoken in a symbol. From the dark
He has sent light. The message that I burned
To give the world is here revealed.
What you have caused this mass of gray to yield,
We, outside prison walls, must draw from men
Behind the bars. The ashes of a soul
We need but gently stir to find the gleam.
Are not earth's purest treasures kept concealed
In her deep breast? Again and yet again
Our searching is rewarded, till the whole
Reality stands master of the dream.
Today your hearth has yielded me a joy
With heavenly meaning, for each man or boy
Whose cause I strive to plead, whose grief is mine,
Is a banked fire which holds a spark divine.
For centuries these holy sparks were hurled
Out on neglected ash-heaps of the world.
Until one came who stirred with tender hands
The grayness and the gloom; who pierced the mass
Of hatred till they said "he understands."
Then prison miracles were brought to pass,
For sparks innumerable he found that filled with light
And comfort many lives, that made the night—
That long, long night of desolate despair—
Seem but a fearful dream, for hope was there,

---

[2] Yes, this is properly formatted as per multiple publications of the original.

ch. ends next p.

And faith in God returned, and self-respect;

Ambition and the will to serve — to be
Good citizens when at last came liberty.

I paused — for it was time for me to go.

The flames had vanished and the fire burned low.

The poet knelt before the embers red—
"You've made my hearth a sacred thing," he said.
"God grant that I may also find the spark
Divine to glorify the dark."

And then beneath the stars I took my way
With a new courage for the men in gray.

Anne P. L. Field.
November, 1915.[3]

---

[3] This poem first appeared in the December 4, 1915, issue of *The Survey* (Volume 35, No. 10, pp. 234–235). We have taken the text that precedes the poem, itself an expanded version of what originally appeared in *The Survey*, from a version syndicated in newspapers after its initial appearance. The Wilford Seymour Conrow (1880-1957) painting at right accompanies the poem in *The Survey* and is, we believe based on many descriptions, a portrait of Canada Blackie. The image caption that appeared with it (also at right) alludes to but does not explicitly state that it is Blackie. However, the figure appears to be wearing a coat similar in style to what Sing Sing prisoners wore at the time, and the medal pinned to his chest appears to bear the Mutual Welfare League emblem. We'd love to see the original!

The artist, W. S. Conrow, is an American painter recently returned from France where his studio fell in the range of military operations — who, like Mrs. Field, has been fired with Mr. Osborne's cause at Sing Sing; and like her has given his work to help interpret it.

My Life Out of Prison
(An Excerpt)

by
Donald Lowrie

Also, his voice had the vibration of fellowship. It was not until I told him I had "done time" that he "loosened up."

"I thought you were a prison reformer," he said; "you know what I mean. You don't look like a guy that's done a long stretch."

During the next hour Jack and I became friends. I have since received several letters from him. The following is a portion of the first one:

"135 State St., Auburn, N. Y.
"April 20, 1914.

"Dear Donald: Yours arrived and received a royal welcome. I sincerely hope this reaches you before you leave St. Louis. I have spent many happy days in that good old town, Don, and hope your visit shall be a happy one also.

"Well, this is a beautiful night, a silver night, and a fitting sequel to the golden day just passed. The sun has been shining nice and warm all day, and just about five o'clock we had a little shower. It lasted just long enough to freshen things up and left a clear blue sky behind. Just like troubles, eh? Sorrow may seem dark and drear for a time, but eventually it brings the sunshine out from the clouds and the sky seems more bright after. Last Friday was the anniversary of my eleventh year in my little niche of shame, and I have seen much and felt more in that time, believe me, Don. But it's all in the bit, and if a fellow is foolish enough to cut to the break in the deck he has no kick coming if the other fellow holds the best hand. And it's only a fool who will not profit by his mistakes. Now, please do not misconstrue this, old man. I do not wish to convey the idea that I have reformed, for I have not reached the "Turn of the Balance"

My Life Out of Prison

After a day in Chicago, visiting friends, I proceeded to Auburn, New York, where I was scheduled to speak at the State prison.

It was the first time I had faced an audience of prisoners, and there were 1400 of them. When I got on my feet I felt nervous; I realized that I had the chance to perhaps make some of them think. I don't know just what I said, but it must have "taken," for I was frequently interrupted by applause, and at the conclusion of the address, besieged with interesting questions. Most of the queries evinced intelligent thought; none were frivolous or irrelevant.

The following day I received a written order from Warden Rattigan to visit the prison at will and to go wherever I wished. "Billy" Duffy, a slim young fellow, serving twelve years, and sergeant-at-arms of the prisoners' Mutual Welfare League, was assigned as my cicerone.[1] We indeed went "everywhere," even into the "jail," the "isolation" ward, and the death chamber. In the latter dreadful place, the guard in charge, after explaining the method of electrocution in detail,

---

[1] Tour guide.

asked me if I cared to sit in the "chair," and when I drew back with a quick declination, seemed surprised.

"Why, all visitors like to do that," he said, half apologetically; "they like to tell their friends that they've sat in the chair."

"But I am thinking of that wretched woman they brought in from Salamanca today," I mumbled. "She's doomed to have her life snuffed out in that thing and she's the mother of children."

"Yes, it's too bad," was the answer. "We've already sent off two women in this State. It's a bad business — a bad business."

"Do you believe in it — in capital punishment?" I asked.

"I certainly don't," he replied. "It's a fierce proposition to have to strap a man in that chair while the priests are praying out loud, and then strip his corpse a few minutes later so the doctors can cut him up."

"So the doctors can cut him up?" I questioned. "What do you mean?"

"Why, it's the law," he replied. "Ev'ry man we send off has to have his brain examined before it's cold."

This was news to me, and interesting.

"How long has that been the law?" I asked.

"Oh, I don't know. Quite a long time."

"And how many 'warm' brains have been examined?" I persisted.

"Couple o' hundred, I guess," was the reply. "Why?"

"Oh, I was just wondering if a murderer's brain had been established," I said, dully. "But, of course, it hasn't or we'd have read scientific articles about it. They're just like you and me, aren't they?"

"Yes, I guess they are," he said, seriously. "I've seen some mighty fine men sent off; men that had it 'on me' for intelligence, and other ways. But they've just passed a law that all executions will be at Sing Sing; we'll soon be rid of the 'chair' here, thank God. I don't sleep well for a week after seeing one of them bodies cut open."

In the "isolation" ward nearby I glimpsed five stolid faces in five "condemned" cells — one of them a Chinaman. Farther on I stopped and chatted with various "incorrigibles." It was significant that the condemned and the "incorrigibles" were celled together. Perhaps the most interesting man I found was Jack Murphy, a lifer, who had been in the prison ten years and in "solitary" two years. He had a mother cat with three kittens in his cell and at first seemed disinclined to talk. But I liked him; he was slender, and his graying hair plenteous.

Also, his voice had the vibration of fellowship. It was not until I told him I had "done time" that he "loosened up."

"I thought you were a prison reformer," he said; "you know what I mean. You don't look like a guy that's done a long stretch."

During the next hour Jack and I became friends. I have since received several letters from him. The following is a portion of the first one:

> "135 State St., Auburn, N.Y.
> "April 20, 1914.

"Dear Donald: Yours arrived and received a royal welcome. I sincerely hope this reaches you before you leave St. Louis. I have spent many happy days in that good old town, Don, and hope your visit shall be a happy one also.

"Well, this is a beautiful night, a silver night, and a fitting sequel to the golden day just passed. The sun has been shining nice and warm all day, and just about five o'clock we had a little shower. It lasted just long enough to freshen things up and left a clear blue sky behind. Just like troubles, eh? Sorrow may seem dark and drear for a time, but eventually it brings the

ch. ends next p.

xxviii   The Story of Canada Blackie

sunshine out from the clouds and the sky seems more bright after. Last Friday was the anniversary of my eleventh year in my little niche of shame, and I have seen much and felt more in that time, believe me, Don. But it's all in the bit, and if a fellow is foolish enough to cut to the break in the deck he has no kick coming if the other fellow holds the best hand. And it's only a fool who will not profit by his mistakes. Now, please do not misconstrue this, old man. I do not wish to convey the idea that I have reformed, for I have not reached the 'Turn of the Balance' yet, but if I do, and perhaps I have a little yearning that I may, why I — well, I hope I can be just about as good as I have been bad. I have been thinking a whole lot since you left me that day and I wish I could meet such men as you every day. It helps, Don. A hearty handclasp and a pleasant smile works wonders in the heart of the man who is down. They say a man can't come back. That's foolish, Don. A knockdown is only a rest which a fellow can have while he is taking the count. He can then come up fresh to renew the fight. Well, I suppose I have tired you with all this prattle, so I will close by wishing you all the beautiful things this world affords. Sincerely yours,

"John E. Murphy, No. 32,378."

"P.S. — I expect the book most any day now. Thank you, Don. Goodnight. Write or drop a card when you can; I shall welcome either.

"Jack."

Today, as you read these words, the man who wrote them is cooped in a stone cell. True, he has a yard — a place about twelve feet square, with walls fifteen feet high, and a netting over the top so that he cannot throw communications to the men on either side — each man in the "isolation" ward

at Auburn has a yard, which means a patch of sky. I know
in my heart that Jack Murphy, Auburn No. 32,378, is a big
man — a big man gone wrong. I didn't intend to write about
him at all, but his personality forced it. I hope the day will
come when he will get his chance. I believe it will.

The Story of Canada Blackie

The Story of Canada Blackie

CHAPTER I

Introducing Canada Blackie

EARLY in the gray dawn of February 26th, 1915, three men went to the electric chair in Sing Sing Prison while "Canada Blackie," himself near death from tuberculosis, lay on his little white bed on the third floor of the warden's house at Sing Sing and whispered this prayer which the watcher by the bedside will never forget.

1

Introducing Canada Blackie

Early in the gray dawn of February 26th, 1915, three men went to the electric chair in Sing Sing Prison while "Canada Blackie," himself near death from tuberculosis, lay on his little white bed on the third floor of the warden's house at Sing Sing and whispered this prayer which the watcher by the bedside will never forget:

> "O God, if I could only be taken instead of those three young men in the full vigor of their strength! There is work for them to do on this earth, even behind the bars, while my course is run. The sand in my hourglass has only a few grains left, and they are rapidly slipping through. But — Thy will be done! and if they are to go and I am to stay, even for a little while, may it be for some great and high purpose. O God, in spite of the past, make the life of each man within the walls count for something! May the passing out of those three brave souls today mean also the passing out of that old medieval law of capital punishment. Bless all my dear pals everywhere."

"Canada Blackie," so called because of his Canadian nativity and his thick raven hair, was one of the most dramatic and picturesque figures in modern criminal annals, and for twelve years was considered the most daring and dangerous convict in New York State. A victim of the stupid brutality of the old prison system — his early and tragic death in his forty-second year, the direct result of its maltreatment, he was also the most triumphant example of the reforming power of the new system of common sense as introduced at Auburn by Mr. Thomas M. Osborne — now warden of Sing Sing — and Warden Rattigan of Auburn,[1] by permission of State Superintendent of Prisons John B. Riley,[2] and now being successfully worked out at Auburn and Sing Sing.

Blackie died a free man. Governor Whitman[3] pardoned him on February 16th, 1915, after hearing from Warden Osborne of the man's desperate illness, and the remarkable story of his change of heart and his service to his fellow prisoners.

Blackie's adventurous career began at an early age. His mother, whom he dearly loved, died when he was a mere lad. In later years, in a letter to a friend, he wrote, "My mother died brokenhearted. Her last thoughts were of me. Her last word my name. When they whispered that I would not be there to kiss her goodbye, her poor heart broke. 'Goldheart' was my pet name for her, and her heart was gold indeed!" In another letter to the same friend he says:

"For years I have been so much alone that sometimes I feel like a tired bird at sea. Tonight, though, after once more reading your letters, I am again a

---

[1] Charles F. Rattigan (1865–1956) was a newspaper publisher who served as warden of Auburn Prison from May 26, 1913, to May 1, 1916, and later as the New York State Superintendent of Prisons, two terms after Riley.

[2] Riley served in that position from 1913 to 1916.

[3] Charles Seymour Whitman (1868–1947) was a lawyer who served as the New York County District Attorney from 1910 to 1914, then became the 41st Governor of New York from 1915 to 1918.

carefree boy at mother's side. Once again I see the dear old homestead resting peacefully upon the hillside. Once more I watch the sun sinking behind the mountains, leaving a trail of violet haze that is good to look upon. Over in the meadowland a silvery throated bird is singing its vesper hymn, and from afar I catch a faint bark from dear old Dan as he drives home the cows for milking. The maple-tops sway gracefully in the soft southland breeze, and all is restful and full of peace. Mother is at the organ playing a soft strain that will linger forever with me. Now she allows her gaze to turn from the music and wander over to me, and I notice that refined look of delicacy which is hers by birthright. Sister is there also. What a loving little angel she was! — always ready to help mother smooth away my little boyhood troubles."

Rebelling at his father's unreasonableness and lack of understanding, the boy Blackie ran away from home and joined a circus troupe, with which for two years he was an aerial performer of considerable skill. Regarding that experience he said:

"I loved the life — it just suited my daredevil temperament. The danger and excitement of it; the thrill of swinging through the air, in silk tights, before a breathless, fascinated throng, twice a day! But it all ended suddenly one night, and I hated it then as much as I had loved it! As I was about to swing toward my woman partner, fifty feet away, my eyes were distracted by the sight of a brilliant yellow feather bobbing up and down in the crowd below. I missed my count, and failed to catch her when she let go of her trapeze, and she fell. I can still hear the sickening crunch of her body as it struck the turf — that was before the day of safety nets — that night I ran away again, but the woman is still living maimed for life — by a yellow feather!"

Recently when asked if he could remember any incident in his childhood tending to start him on his life of crime, he replied:

"Yes, I can tell you of one, and when you're speaking on prison reform this story will illustrate how all these questions of education and child-welfare and prison reform are inter-related. When I was seven years old I attended a little country school of about twenty-four pupils. The teacher was just a slip of a girl scarcely out of her teens, and without any interest in her work. She was engaged to be married, and when she wasn't twirling her engagement ring and gazing into space, she was reading *The Duchess*![4] I was a quick-witted kid. I never had to study very hard to get my lessons, and I had sized up that teacher. She got on my nerves. I never could stand stupidity in anything — much less in a woman, so one day when we were all out for recess, I called a bunch of the kids over in a corner of the yard and said: 'I'll bet you a round of peppermint sticks that I can give teacher a wrong answer in geography and get away with it.' They took me up and dared me, and when the class was called, teacher, with that far-away look in her eyes, asked me to bound the State of Maine. I stood up as cool as you please and rattled off in one breath: 'Maine is bounded on the north by the Pacific Ocean, on the south by the Gulf of Mexico, on the east by New Jersey and on the west by New York,' and all that teacher did was to yawn and say, 'Next, bound Connecticut!' From that minute I was the real teacher

[4] *The Duchess* was first serialized in 1887 by Irish novelist Margaret Wolfe Hungerford (1855–1897) under the pen name "The Duchess," which she used for most of her published works.

of that school. I had tasted my first sense of power, and I had discovered how half asleep most people are, and how easy it is to fool them! I was the leader of those twenty-four kids from that day — and I got the peppermint sticks, too!"

A few years later Blackie became the leader of a gang of young crooks, most of whom were several years older than he. He was the brains of the band. He would think out a plan for a robbery like a general planning a great battle, and then direct its carrying out to the smallest detail.

Blackie became a famous cracksman[5] — "the whitest of yeggmen," as his pals called him. He used to laugh and say:

"Yes, I always claimed to be a direct descendant of old John Yegg. Who was John Yegg? Why, John was the greatest gypsy bandit that ever roved, and his followers were called 'Yeggmen.' He was a game and fearless old man who stopped at nothing. It seemed grand to me then to be an outlaw. I knew no authority, and took pride in recklessness. The greatest sensation I ever had was standing with a loaded revolver over an engineer's heart, and ordering him to slow down an express train for *me!* Gee! that was some sensation! Penalty? — no man intent on a job ever thinks of the penalty. Of course, somewhere back in his subconscious mind there's the idea of being caught and penalty, but in the excitement of the moment he forgets it and knows no law."

In April, 1903, Blackie was sentenced to life imprisonment for participating in a raid on a country bank in which the watchman was killed. Two members of his gang went to the electric chair, and a third is still serving a life-sentence. Blackie was sent to Clinton — the prison, as someone has

---

[5] Safecracker; burglar.

ch. ends next p.

vividly described it, — "on the bleak hilltop of Dannemora,
up above Plattsburg; the pen for convicts spewed out by
the gentler prisons."[6] During the first seven years he had
a perfect record. His behavior was exemplary, but the iron
and stone entered his very soul and his nerves were shattered
by the thousand and one petty rules and humiliations of
the stupid system under which he was compelled to exist.
Finally he could *exist* no longer — he must *live* — and he
determined to escape. With Blackie determination meant
action. By that baffling underground method which has been
the bane of all prison officials, he obtained a quantity of
dynamite and buried it in the prison yard, with the inten-
tion of blowing up the entire north end of the cell-block.
The scheme was disclosed by a stool-pigeon,[7] and Blackie
entered solitary confinement. After several months of this
living death he made another desperate attempt to escape.
By the same underground method he secured a piece of
gas-pipe from which he fashioned a crude revolver, which
he charged with powder made by grinding up the heads of
matches and by scraping the sides of matchboxes. "It was
exciting work making that revolver," he told a friend, "and it
took months to save enough matches. I set her off by a trigger
attached to a piece of string. Sometimes she refused to work,
but it did the business all right the night I needed it. I shot a
guard through the shoulder — though I got twelve months
in a dark cell for doing it." He was taken to Plattsburg for
trial, and there Judge Riley, now the state superintendent of
prisons, gave him an additional sentence of ten years. He was
returned to Dannemora and kept in a dark cell for one year
more — twenty months in all. There was no window, and
an extra heavy wooden door was put over the steel entrance
door, so that by no chance could he escape or communicate
with others.

[6] Dannemora and Plattsburg are cities located in Clinton County, New York.
[7] Informant.

Only a man of Blackie's indomitable courage and endurance could have survived this treatment, and he was obliged
to invent schemes to retain his reason. When questioned
about those terrible months, he said:

"No one who has not been through a similar experience can imagine the horror, and to me with my high-
strung nature it was hell! I had to work hard to keep my
mind. I used to call back every bit of stray verse I had
ever learned, and would spend days piecing together
some long-forgotten stanza. I remember the great
difficulty I had in recalling a line in 'Casabianca.'[8] It
was two weeks before I got it, but it finally came. I got
back every line of 'Locksley Hall,'[9] and a good deal
of 'Childe Harold,'[10] as well as a lot of hymns that my
mother taught me when I was a little boy. I always was
an enthusiast over poetry.

"I tore off the buttons from my undershirt and
tossed them into the darkness, and then would spend
hours groping for them. It took me three days once to
find one button, for it had rolled into a crack between
the doors, but I got it one morning when they swept
out the cell. Getting that button was an achievement.
It was like finishing the Pyramids or completing a long
and hazardous journey."

[8] A poem by English poet Felicia Dorothea Hemans (1793–1835).
[9] A poem written by Alfred Tennyson (1809–1892) in 1835 and published in
his collection *Poems* (1842).
[10] *Childe Harold's Pilgrimage* is a long narrative poem in four parts written
by Lord Byron (1788–1824).

2

Blackie at Auburn Prison

The day came when it was thought advisable to transfer Blackie to Auburn. The keepers at Dannemora knew that the dynamite was still concealed somewhere in the yard, and they were all afraid that in some secret way, known only to the underworld, Blackie would instruct others to use it. He was sent to Auburn, blind in one eye through atrophy of the optic nerve, brought on by the darkness, and already the victim of the tuberculosis which caused his death. Arriving at Auburn he was at once put again into solitary confinement, in the isolation block of cells with the condemned men. It was a feast of liberty compared with the dark cell at Dannemora, for the isolation cells at Auburn have beds and toilet arrangements, and each cell has a little yard in front — a space twelve feet square, with walls fifteen feet high, and a netting over the top, so that no communication can be thrown to a neighbor, but where a man can exercise, and see "the little tent of blue that prisoners call the sky!"

Here he spent two more years, still untamed and rebellious toward the prison officials. But his attitude toward the men caged in the isolation block was one of deep interested friendship. Many a man on the eve of his execution was comforted and sustained by Blackie's brave words and cheering voice, and many were the letters written by him to the loved ones of some wretched man facing the chair.

Once a boy of twenty-one came in condemned to die. This boy's mother was very religious and her heart was agonized. Blackie knew the lad and his story and he yearned to comfort the mother, remembering his own mother so vividly. Among the lad's possessions was a hymn book that his mother had sent him, so one night Blackie wrote some verses about that little hymn book, and told the lad to send them to his mother, which he did, and the mother thought her own boy had written them. These are the verses:

MOTHER'S HYMN BOOK

One day as I sat yearning for happy days
    of yore,
The captain with a bunch of mail stopped
    just outside my door;
He handed me a package tied with a
    ribbon frail,
A simple little message, but to me a
    golden tale,
For I found inside the wrapper a hymn-
    book old and worn,
Which mother used to sing from before
    her boy was born,
And sister on the fly leaf wrote lovingly
    to say —
"This is the book, dear Jack, from which
    our mother used to pray."
I opened it at random, and there before
    my eyes
Was that dear hymn she loved so well,
    "His Mansions in the Skies" —
I slowly turned the pages, each verse a

message gold,
And read where Jesus welcomed back
    the lost ones to the fold,
And gathered up the sunbeams that help
    to brighten life,
For there'll be no dark valleys; all joy
    instead of strife.
So I'll trim the lights along my way, and
    keep them burning bright,
And throw a life-line where I can, for
    mother says it's right.
And if perchance some weary soul I'll
    help along life's way,
Then God has blessed this little book
    from which she used to pray.

They were read in the village church on the following Sunday, with the result that steps were immediately taken to secure a commutation of sentence — steps which eventually proved successful.

Blackie had a mother cat and three kittens in his cell at Auburn, and in telling a friend how he acquired the pets, he said: "One night when the guard brought my supper, an old gray cat strayed in. The place was alive with rats, so cats were allowed. I was so excited I couldn't eat, for that old gray tabby was the first warm living thing I had touched for over five years. I talked to her as if she were human. I tried to hypnotize her so she would remember me and come back, and she did; she understood and became my friend — she knew my desperate need — animals know such things sometimes better than men. She used to sleep on my pillow and I'd put my face close up to her soft fur and be purred to sleep. I can tell you that no music in all the world was ever so transcending as that cat's purring was to my starved ears. I used to save some of my supper for her every night — and

ch. ends p. 14

then one memorable day she presented me with three pretty little kittens, which I helped her bring up and educate.

"Tabby's maternal instincts were not very deep, I'm afraid, for long before the kittens were old enough to fend for themselves she deserted them. I loved them dearly, and couldn't bear to see them die of starvation, so I used to take a small piece of my slice of bread and chew it until it was soft pulp, then feed it to the kittens. I also shared my cup of water with them, and on that meager fare they grew into sizable cats."

One of the most significant events in Blackie's life in Auburn was his meeting with Donald Lowrie, the man who spent ten years in San Quentin prison and who is the author of that soul-stirring book, *My Life in Prison* — the book that prompted Mr. Osborne to spend a week as an inmate of Auburn prison. A graphic account of the initial meeting of these two men is to be found in Lowrie's recently published book, *My Life Out of Prison*.[1]

Blackie and Lowrie became firm friends and corresponded regularly. Lowrie when a guest of Mr. Osborne's at Auburn, on visiting the prison, received a written order from Warden Rattigan to go wherever he pleased, so he paid a visit to the isolation ward and became particularly impressed with Blackie's personality. Permission has been given to quote from Blackie's letter which appears in *My Life Out of Prison*.

"Dear Donald:

"Yours arrived and received a royal welcome. I sincerely hope this reaches you before you leave St. Louis. I have spent many happy days in that good old town, Don, and hope your visit will be a happy one also.

"Well, this is a beautiful night, a silver night and a

---

[1] Lowrie provides a more detailed account of his time spent with Blackie at Sing Sing in his book *Back in Prison—Why?*, whose relevant chapters we have included later in this book.

fitting sequel to the golden day just passed. The sun has been shining nice and warm all day and just about five o'clock we had a little shower. It lasted just long enough to freshen things up, and left a clear blue sky behind. Just like troubles, eh? Sorrow may seem dark and drear for a time, but eventually it brings the sunshine out from the clouds, and the sky seems more bright after. Last Friday was the anniversary of my eleventh year in my little niche of shame, and I have seen much and felt more in that time, believe me, Don. But it's all in the bit, and if a fellow's foolish enough to cut to the break in the deck, he has no kick coming if the other fellow holds the best hand, and it's only a fool who will not profit by his mistakes. Now, please do not misconstrue this, old man. I do not wish to convey the idea that I have reformed, for I have not reached the 'Turn of the Balance' yet, but if I do, and perhaps I have a little yearning that I may, why I — well, I hope I can be just about as good as I have been bad. I have been thinking a whole lot since you left me that day and I wish I could meet such men as you every day. It helps, Don; a hearty handclasp and a pleasant smile work wonders in the heart of the man who is down.

"They say a man can't come back. That's foolish, Don. A knockdown is only a rest which a fellow can have while he is taking the count. He can then come up fresh to renew the fight. Well, I suppose I have tired you with all this prattle, so I will close by wishing you all the beautiful things this world affords."

In May 1913, five months before he spent his week in Auburn prison, Mr. Osborne met Blackie. Mr. Rattigan had just been made warden and Mr. Osborne visited the isolation block with him, and they stopped in front of Blackie's cell. There they saw a tall gaunt man, considerably over six feet in height, with the familiar tuberculosis stoop. He had a finely

ch. ends next p.

shaped head covered with thick, wavy black hair, streaked with gray, a strong chin and jaw, with a firm well-molded mouth, and a pair of fearless hazel eyes, the direct gaze of which seemed to penetrate a man's inmost soul. Extraordinary eyes they were — changing with every mood — the eyes of a master mind, revealing an almost uncanny power as they flashed out from under their heavy black brows. Noticeable also were his hands — with unusually long, flexible fingers and deep palms; inventive, capable, determined hands which he used continually, emphasizing his vivid conversation with a thousand gestures.

In regard to this meeting, Mr. Osborne has written, "I did not know who the prisoner was, and did not associate him with the dangerous man of whom I had heard. Mr. Rattigan introduced us and then passed on to the next cell, while I stopped to chat. After we had spoken a few words I said to him, 'How long a term have you?' He answered, 'Life, and ten years' — then seeing the corners of my mouth beginning to twitch, he added, 'Does seem a little superfluous, doesn't it?'

"It was the next month, in June I think, that I visited him in his cell and we talked of prison reform."

3

Blackie on Prison Reform

It was after this second visit that Blackie gave Mr. Osborne the following extraordinary notes of his ideas on the subject of their conversation.

"If I wish to move forward out of shadow into sunshine, out of wrong into right, how must I make the start?

"To answer this question fully would require a large volume, but a brief statement will sometimes suffice. Someone has said, 'As a man thinketh, so is he.'[1] Taking this as a fact, I must therefore make my start from the point of right thought. To do this, though, I require some help, for I find that under existing regulations I cannot bring myself to think as a normal person should. My environment is foreign to my nature. I am compelled to live and work with my fellow man, but outside of what conversation my work requires I am prohibited from talking. This barrier from all social intercourse with my fellow man has a tendency

[1] Proverbs 23:7

to unfit me for my life to come in the outer world. Expression is life. A beautiful thought unexpressed dies. A painting must have proper expression before it is a recognized work of art. A man cannot very well demonstrate his good or bad qualities unless given a chance to do so. How can anyone tell whether I am fit to take my place in the outer world and live as it was intended I should live, unless I have been given a chance to demonstrate my worth while here?

"Some years ago I lived in a small railroad division town. There was no place of amusement, and the only place the men had to pass their spare time was in the saloon, until some one fitted up a room in the depot and started a Y.M.C.A. The larger part of the men spent their time in that room after that. Why doesn't some bright fellow in prison start something like that? In the event of such, the men so inclined could gather to discuss the topics of the day. There could be debates, lectures and ethics, in fact everything which has a tendency to uplift the men, could be worked out in that room. There could also be a quiet room for those who wish to read or write. I know many men who could support their loved ones were they only allowed the privilege to sell their articles to a publisher. There could also be the hall privilege. A man wishing to spend an evening with a friend could, if his conduct merited it, take his chair and sit by his friend's door. All these privileges would be eagerly looked forward to after the day of silence in the shop. If silence must be maintained in the shop, why not give the men a chance in the evenings to fit themselves for an honest life when they are set free? To do these things would require more night officers of course, but the good derived from them would be well worth the little expense attached.

"In one of the western prisons there is a swimming

pool where the men can bathe. When a man finishes his work he takes his towel, soap, etc., and leaves the shop to take his bath. No officer is required, as the men maintain the discipline and it is well kept, you may be sure. In Columbus the men are paid for all work turned out after their allotted day's work is finished. The money consists of checks. These the men keep themselves, and can use them to purchase what is allowed. They also have hall privileges. All these things help to uplift. The men work better, behave better, think better thoughts and so are better fitted to take their place in the world once more. A man will show his best side when rewarded. Threaten and bully him and the chances are he will remain in the same old rut. Over in Toronto, Canada, the Central prison works four hundred men on a farm of twelve hundred acres. These men are well behaved — only four out of a transient population of a thousand tried to escape, and not one-half the number came back to prison that used to under the old inside system. The road building in this State has so far proved a success. Why not extend it? If it gives satisfaction to a few, it will to the many. Cooperation is what is required in all prisons. Give a man a chance to help himself and in return he will help others. The prisons for centuries have been run by repression. What has it accomplished? Society's pocketbook could best answer that question. And that reminds us of the question of self-support. The State for years has had to support her prisoners. It is nearly time now that some way should be devised whereby the prisoner could become self-supporting, and at the same time be enabled to add to the support of his family. Crime would greatly decrease if such a law could be enacted. To take the breadwinner from his family, and leave them in poverty and want would be the proper thing to do if society were looking to

ch. ends p. 22

make an industry of crime. Since I came to prison I witnessed a striking illustration of how crime increases. Some moving pictures were being shown where a man was sent to prison — his wife, the only support now of their child of seven, became sick shortly after the father had left them. The little boy, to procure medicine, etc., for his mother, scaled the wall surrounding a rich man's mansion, and took an armful of flowers from the garden beds. These he sold to passersby on the street. Several trips the little fellow made before the inevitable came. He was caught, taken before the owner and was about to be handed to a policeman, when the daughter of the house happened into the room. To her the boy told his story. Upon investigation the lad's story proved to be true, and, of course, that brought about a happy ending in that case, but how is it in most all other cases where there is no lady bountiful to intercede? The boy goes to the reformatory, and under their present systems, reformatories are busy hives of industry, where boys are turned out fit pupils for any life of crime they may choose. This one prison alone proves that. It is safe to say seventy or eighty percent of the inmates of this institution are graduates from some reformatory. The percentage runs high in most all prisons, also. The boy who is sent to a reform school simply because he is a truant is placed with the boy who is there for theft. From him he gets his first lesson — the rest is known by all.

"Some time ago, a career of crime was cut short by the law. The man received his start from an institution where children are sent who have disobeyed in some manner. From there he went to the reformatory, then to prison, and, finally, to his death as decreed by the law.

"Had he been paroled when a youngster, instead of being sent to that institution, where he mingled with young thieves, the State might have been saved that execution. Judge Lindsey, of Denver, is paroling boys from his court every day.[2] He takes the youngster into his private room, talks to him in a fatherly manner, gains his confidence, and a promise to live better, then sends him out to keep that promise. The boy never sees the inside of the reformatory, and is all the better for not doing so. Some day the boy will be a respected citizen. Had he been sent away when his mind and will were in a wayward condition, his chances of becoming a criminal were large.

"'Familiarity breeds contempt' they say. Place a young boy in a reformatory and he soon loses his fear of state prison. This is also true in the case of first offenders who come to the prisons. Had they been paroled before they had a chance to get hardened to the life, there would have been less repeaters for the State to contend with.

"With all the prisons in New York State, the officials find it hard to make room for the steady increase of population. The prisons are so congested now that some of the men have to sleep out in the halls. In some cases two men have to exist in one little cell that is not large enough for one. How can the State expect to turn out good men under such trying circumstances? If a man can rise above a condition like that, he must be made of excellent stuff, and it is very seldom that that kind of man comes to prison.

"If environment makes the man, and reform is really sought after, then make the environment as it should be. Give the men a chance to prove their worth. Help them to think right and you will find that the majority will respond to right treatment. That a great deal of

[2] Benjamin Barr Lindsey (1869–1943) was known as the father of juvenile law. He established the first juvenile court in Denver, Colorado, and was known for his advocacy for juvenile rights, women's rights, and workers' rights.

injustice exists in the world is true, and that many who are strong are taking advantage of multitudes that are weak is also true, but there is a peaceful way to remedy a lot of this if the people can only be brought to look upon things as they should be, and not as they are. There is no remedy in sight so far that the State can adopt that will make the convict self-supporting; but each individual interested in prison reform can so relate himself to the work in hand, that the financial increase to the State, and the problem of recompense and reward to the convict for his labor will be solved. To do this, no under-value nor over-value should be placed on his work. Today the market for prison-made articles is limited. Would it not be better for all concerned if the prisoner had access to the general market? This can only be accomplished by giving him a fair wage for his labor, and make him support himself out of that wage. If a man is receiving all that he deserves, he will make himself more deserving, and will, of course, turn out better work than is at present being manufactured inside prison walls, and the State will receive the general market price for the article. Worth is what the world recognizes, and to make an article worth selling, you will have to pay to have it made. The average person who thinks he is being underpaid will not take the proper interest in his work, nor can he be expected to do so. The man who thinks he is not getting a fair deal will not reveal himself as he really is; his real nature is misdirected in anything he undertakes, and everybody is deceived, for he will continually fight against putting his best efforts into his work. This, of course, keeps up a friction between him and those whose interests it is to have good work turned out. On the other hand, if he is rewarded for his labor, all these troubles will be cleared away and everyone will be benefited. The State cannot lose by treating her prisoners fairly, and the prisoner is more contented and will live up to the rules when he knows that by turning out a good day's work he is not only benefiting himself, but is also supporting his wife and little ones who are, when we come to look at it rightly, the real sufferers. No man can do what really is right when he knows his dear ones are in want. And right here I ask you to put yourself in the prisoner's place and ask yourself what would your thoughts be in that case?

"And now just a word in regard to uplifting the prisoner and giving him a chance to look upon things as he should. Some people claim that environment makes the man. If this is true, then why not make prison environment as it should be and not as it is? There is no more danger in giving a convict an opportunity to get education so that he may be a good citizen, than there is in holding him back and allowing him to degrade himself so that he will remain worthless. This does not apply to school education, solely. A man can be a good scholar and still be a pessimist. What is needed, but is sadly lacking, is some way by which the prisoner can be taught to look upon his incarceration in an optimistic manner.

"When a man first comes to prison, he is given a rule-book — after reading it through, he comes to this threat: 'Any infraction of these rules will be punished accordingly.' Why not let it read: 'Prisoners obeying these rules will be *rewarded* accordingly.' That would make the man look upon that set of rules in a little brighter light, instead of driving the steel home to his heart as they now do to some men right on the start of their sentences.

"Another thing which would be a large factor in the behavior of the men, would be to grade them according to their merits. Many socially inclined men get into trouble by being compelled to mix with constant grumblers. This latter class should be kept by themselves. If this was done the good men in the shops would very soon get rid of any undesirables, and in a short while the men themselves would see that discipline would be maintained, and that one thing is the secret of success in prison, providing that the man in charge is a person who has full control of himself; for to control others, we must first learn the lesson of self-control. I have known many officers who have gained the respect of the men in their charge simply by using good judgment. That kind of man seems to know how to handle men. Some time ago one of our greatest penologists wrote an article on paroling all first offenders at the door of the prison. This man seems to know what he is advocating. Oftentimes you will find unexpected good qualities in men from whom you looked for naught but evil, but these good points he will not show to any but the one he considers the right person, and for all of us there is that 'right person.'"

These notes are very remarkable, especially so, as coming from a man in solitary confinement — a man who, as he wrote Lowrie, had then not yet reached the "turn of the balance."

4

Blackie and Mr. Osborne

Blackie and Mr. Osborne became close friends by the time the latter had served his week in Auburn prison. He often visited Blackie, who took a keen interest in his experiment and in the formation of the Mutual Welfare League.[1] On one of Mr. Osborne's visits, Blackie, wretchedly ill and suffering, had been rather reticent and morose. After his friend had gone he realized how coldly he had treated him, so he wrote the following letter by way of reparation:

"After you left me yesterday, I felt sad and very much ashamed of myself — ashamed to know that I wounded your feelings. Yes, I did hurt you, *mon ami*,[2] I know it. Being somewhat sensitive myself, I too, felt it, and can therefore fully realize how my reticent manner must have seemed to you. And I hope

[1] After Osborne spent a week as an inmate in Auburn prison, he developed, with the assistance of Auburn's inmates, a system of prison self-government to be instituted and operated by the prisoners themselves. Osborne recounts his time as an inmate and the creation of the M.W.L. in his 1914 book *Within Prison Walls*.

[2] Translated from French: my friend.

you will believe me when I say that I am sorry, very, very sorry.

"You have been so good, so kind — *mon ami* — that it hurts me to know that I should be the one to cause you any displeasure. I have no excuse to offer for myself, but I do sincerely hope that you will kindly forgive me. Just after you went away I picked up *The Virginian* and came to the passage where 'The Virginian,' in speaking to his friend said, 'I ain't religious, I know that, but I ain't unreligious,' and I know that too.[3] There's one kind of religion that I respect when I meet it. It is not praying or preaching that has ever caught me and made me ashamed of myself, but one or two people I have known that never said a superior word to me. They thought more of me than I deserved and that made me behave better than I naturally wanted to. And if ever I was to have a son or somebody I set store by, I would wish their lot to be to know one or two good folks mighty well, men or women. And so it is with me, *mon ami*, I, too, would like to be able to hold the respect of one or two good folks mighty well. Some day, perhaps, we shall get to know one another a little better, then you will understand. In the meantime, please try to think of me as well as you possibly can. In writing this I feel that you will know that my contrition is sincere, for I think you know that I am not a sycophant,[4] also that I am not a dissembler. And I am proud to say that I have never, knowingly, betrayed a confidence.

"The Stork came and left me three little baby kittens, 'Nona' named after 'Anona,' you know, and 'Mona,' after 'Ramona,' and I suppose I must call the other one 'Tom Brown.' But I hope he never has to put in a night

---

[3] Those lines can be found in Chapter 18 of the 1902 novel *The Virginian: A Horseman of the Plains* by Owen Wister (1860-1938).

[4] One who flatters in order to gain favor or advantage.

in the cooler! Now do not tell the ladies or they will be down here with a ribbon-shower, sure. Baby blue, is it not? One thing, though, you can do if you will. That is, give my sincere respects to your daughter-in-law, and also to those brave little women who had the courage to go over into the women's prison and do their bit like majors. I have heard what they are doing for the girls over there and they are both little empresses. Well, you must be tired now, so I will close by wishing you all that is good and beautiful. Goodnight, *mon ami*. God bless you and yours is the sincere prayer of one who would like to be worthy of the friendship of such good people."

✲

On the 2nd of June 1914, Blackie invited Mr. Osborne to come into his cell, remarking that he "had something to give the warden." As Mr. Osborne sat there on the bed chatting, Blackie took down a tin box of talcum-powder, and from it extracted a small object tightly bound in a cotton rag. Unwinding this covering he produced a key which he handed to him with the remark: "That key unlocks my cell door. I made it myself, and intended using it to escape." Then he added, with pardonable pride, "I'm the only man in this prison who could have made that!" And he told how, when Lowrie had visited him, the key had been tested and the door was open. He had to hold his foot against the door to keep it shut. Then he stooped, and from another hiding-place, drew out an ugly knife, also of home manufacture, which he presented to Mr. Osborne with the words: "I intended to use that, too—" and then added — "I want you to give those to the warden and tell him that I appreciate so deeply what he

ch. ends p. 30

and you are trying to do for the men here, that he need have no further anxiety about me, for I'm going straight."

The Mutual Welfare League for self-government had already been established in Auburn with splendid results. The men had been allowed the freedom of the yard three times, beginning with Decoration Day,[5] when they had athletic sports. On June 3rd, after Mr. Osborne had told Warden Rattigan what Blackie had said and done, permission was given him to take Blackie out in the yard. Blackie was among his fellowmen again for the first time in five years. The best description of that experience is given in the following letter sent to Donald Lowrie:

"June 3rd, 1914.

"Dear Friend Don:

"The above is the date of my new birthday. After five years of a living death in solitary, I have been resurrected again — making my second time on earth, as it were. So you see I was right when I said, 'A man can come back.' On the evening of the third Mr. Osborne came to my door and as the officer who accompanied him inserted the key to spring my lock, Mr. Osborne said, 'Get your coat and cap, old fellow, I want you to come with me and see something worthwhile.' Knowing that the men had recently been given the liberty of the yard, I, of course, immediately divined the kindness about to be bestowed. I at first felt inclined to say that I could not accept the invitation, knowing, though, that it was extended in all kindness. My reason for wanting to refuse was because I felt that I would feel too keenly the embarrassment that comes to one when suddenly placed among his fellowmen after so long an absence. Mr. Osborne would not, however,

[5] The original name for Memorial Day, which is observed on the last Monday of May in the United States.

4. Blackie and Mr. Osborne 27

take no for an answer, and kindly insisted that I should
put on my coat, he helping me with it, and chatting
pleasantly all the time. This I knew was to put me at
ease. That's another of the many fine characteristics
this big man possesses, Don, — he makes one feel at
home with him right from the start.

"After traversing the corridor of the isolation
building, we came to the double-locked doors — two
of them — which lead directly into the main prison
yard. As we stepped into the pure air I felt as though
I wanted to bite chunks out of it, but the first deep
inhale made me so dizzy that I actually believe I would
have staggered had I not taken myself into firm control.
On rounding the end of the cloth-shop, we came into
full view of the most wonderful, as well as beautiful,
sight I have ever seen in prison — or outside either, for
that matter. I hardly know how to describe this sight;
but picture to yourself, if you possibly can, fourteen
hundred men turned loose in a beautiful park. For
years previous to this good work now being promoted
by Mr. Osborne and the prison officials, these same
men whom I now see running in and out among beautiful flower-beds and playing like a troop of innocent
boys just out of school, had been harnessed, as it were,
to the machines in their respective shops, without even
the privilege of saying goodnight or good morning to
their nearest neighbor. But what a wonderful change
has come to pass! Instead of the prison pallor and
haunted look which once predominated, I now notice
smiling eyes, and that clean look which exhilarating
exercise in the pure air always brings to the face.

"When Mr. Osborne and I reached the lower end of
the park, he invited me to stand where we could get a
full view of everything. Among the first things I noticed
was a ring of the boys formed around something,
I could not see what. Mr. Osborne, in answer to my

ch. ends p. 30

question, said it was a party of Italian lads, waltzing. Just then someone stepped out of the ring, leaving a space through which I could see the boys dancing to their hearts' content. And now my attention was drawn toward a young fellow who was stepping up briskly to shake hands and congratulate me on my new lease of life.

"Just a word about Billy — Billy Duffy being his name. He is an exceptionally bright young fellow, as his rank of sergeant-at-arms of the Mutual Welfare League denotes. Billy is very fond of athletic sports, and is no novice in the manly art. He is also, I'm told, a warm friend of Tom S——. I congratulate S——.

"Several of the boys are now waiting to greet me. Billy, noticing this, turns to chat with Mr. Osborne so as to give them their turn. We are quite a crowd by this time, everyone laughing and joking. Someone suggests that we walk up to the other end of the park. Billy, hearing this, says, 'Yes, come on, old man, it will do you good.' I glance over to Mr. Osborne. He smilingly nods consent. So away we go, he joining the party, also. On the way up the walk, I shake hands with many of the boys, who come running up to extend a kind greeting. Some birthday, eh, Don? All along the line we pass bunches of the fellows, some dancing, others playing stringed instruments, and out on the lawn are hundreds throwing hand ball. Arriving at the upper end of the park, we all go over to lounge on the lawn. I wish I could convey to you the feeling that came to me as I felt the green yielding grass under my feet. I felt as though I wanted to roll right over; and when you stop to consider that I have not had any grass to stretch out on for over twelve years, you can readily understand my feelings. After spending a very happy evening, the bugle sounded assembly. Mr. Osborne, who had left us some time before to chat here and there with others, now hunted me up and said, 'Come along, old chap, I want you to see how nice the boys march in.' By the time we reached the steps of one of the buildings from which we had an excellent view of everything, the men were in their respective places. On both sides of the park the men had formed in double columns on the smooth concrete walks. This gives each man a full view of the beautiful flowerbeds and Old Glory floating in her place at the top of the pole. When the men are all in place, there comes a sudden hush, and then from away up on the extreme right-hand corner from where we stand comes the sweet strain of 'The Star Spangled Banner' and as the flag dips her 'Good Night, Boys' and is slowly lowered, each inmate and officer bares his head in all honor to her colors. The music ceases, and I hear in a soft voice, 'All right, Joe' and Joe, an inmate and delegate of the League, just as softly gives his command, ''Bout face.' His company turns as one man; and then another soft, 'Forward, march,' and away they swing into their cell halls in true military style. After watching several companies run in, Mr. Osborne and I started back to where I belong. In doing this we have to pass between two lines of hundreds of men. As we reach about midway, the boys start a hand clapping. They all recognize the kindness Mr. Osborne has bestowed upon me, and show him their appreciation in this manner; and to me their hearty, 'goodnight, Jack, cheer up, old man,' coming from all down the line, was good to hear. Arriving at my quarters, Mr. Osborne extends his hand and bids me a pleasant 'goodnight' and thus ends my birthday into a new and I hope a better life. Big man? You bet, Don. Tell it to all the good folks out there, won't you?

"Oh, yes! I nearly forgot a very important event. As Mr. Osborne and I were talking, a young fellow came running up and said, 'Mr. Osborne, I wish you would try to understand about that coat. Truly I meant no harm.' Mr. Osborne turned a smiling face to the lad and said, 'It's all right, my boy, I know.' The young fellow thanked him, then scampered back to his play. Truly this man holds us all in the palm of his hand. The incident of the coat must have been trivial — left it where it should not be, or something like that — but that young fellow's sense of honor compelled him to make an apology; and I thought, if they think the little things important enough to ask forgiveness for, it's a certainty that they will be very careful and hesitate before committing anything serious. And that young fellow's attitude expresses, *I feel sure*, the sentiment of all now domiciled in this old battered ship of state, which is at last being steered into calm waters by the most efficient of pilots. With you on the Pacific Coast and our big men on the Atlantic, this good work is going to spread like a prairie on fire. We in Auburn are being very closely watched now, and speculation is rife as to the outcome of this endeavor. But I am positive it will be a success, as the men realize that if it is, it will not be long before every prison in the country will take it up.

"Sometime I will tell you how Mr. Osborne has left his beautiful home, loved ones, etc., and voluntarily allowed himself to be quarantined in here for perhaps weeks. We are having a few cases of scarlet fever, but the doctors have it well under check. Still, no one can come or go. He knew this was about to happen, but left everything beautiful behind so as to be right here in touch with his good work.

"Well, I am tired, so will close and turn in. I hope I have not tired you also, Don, with all this; but it's my birthday, old fellow, and I wanted to share it with you."

5
Blackie and the League

Three weeks later, about the last of June, Blackie was released from solitary confinement and placed among the regular prisoners. He was almost immediately made an assistant sergeant-at-arms of the League, by Billy Duffy, and in July he was elected a delegate and placed on the executive committee. He became a great power for good in Auburn prison. He had admirable ideas on the subject of prison reform, and his brilliant qualities of mind, coupled with his genius for leadership, soon made him a prominent figure. By September he was one of the most trusted men, both by officials and inmates, in the prison. He was thinking and planning night and day how best he could further the interests of the League. Blackie had come to have a great loyal love for "Tom Brown" as Mr. Osborne was affectionately called by all the inmates, and wrote him long, friendly letters, from which the following selections are taken. The "Billy" referred to is Billy Duffy, already mentioned as sergeant-at-arms.

*

"August 25th, 1914.

"Dearest Friend:

"Billy was kind enough to allow me to read your beautiful letter. It, of course, is needless for me to say that I appreciate your loving words as well as he — and the others. Mr. Osborne, you haven't made any mistake in Billy. Could you have only been here that afternoon when he was trying to answer yours, you would have had a look into that big fellow's *big heart*. He wrote page after page only to tear them up and start over again. He wanted to express his very soul I believe, but could not do so on paper. After repeated efforts he turned to me and said, with moisture in his eyes, 'Blackie, I just can't write to Tom. I don't know what I'm turning into. I think I'm getting chicken-hearted, and instead of being a human being I'm beginning to think I should be given a harp and take my place among the angels.' This was not said in an irreverent manner, believe me. You know he can be serious at times — and that was one of the times. He came and pulled me out of my little niche in the wall to show me your letter and I confess that both of us fell down while trying to answer it. I'm alone now. He went over to the southern catacombs, and I suppose repeated his afternoon performance trying to write you what he considered good enough to interest you. It's too bad you did not meet him earlier in his life. You could have molded him into a president — or better — for he has the stuff in him that men are made of. Your executive abilities coupled with your strength and personality, plus Billy's staying qualities, would be the stepping-stones to any height. Everything is lovely here, and we are all going to be good until you come back home to us once more. Of course, we miss you very much, but are glad you are enjoying a much needed rest with your friends. I had a beautiful letter from your sister. Also one from Donald Lowrie, but you shall read them all if you wish. Nice article in *The Outlook*.[1] Well, I've tired you, I suppose, so will say goodnight. Don't fall off any mountains! Regards from all the boys.

"P. S. Billy says 'Sure the north wing can have the cup — *if they win it.*'"

✳

"September 5th, 1914.

"Just read your note to Billy. He has sent a telegram which you must have e'er[2] this. He ran away from us to write it, for we all wanted to say something. Had he allowed us to send all the messages we wished the telegram would have been a book. Now get well, *mon ami.* Gee! we can't stand for all our friends to be laid up. First it was the warden, then Donald and now yourself. We all want you to have a good rest, of course, but sick! No! no! never! Be cheerful, dear friend. You know my old motto — '*Nil desperandum*' never despair — it's a big help for sick folks — and others. Billy says, 'If Tom comes back he can have the cup and banner, Oh, the whole damn South Hall if he will only show up hale and hearty.' Best wishes and sincere hopes for a speedy recovery from all."

✳

[1] Based on the date, likely a reference to "The New Freedom at Auburn Prison" by Orlando F. Lewis, General Secretary of the Prison Association of New York, that appeared in the August 15, 1914, edition of *The Outlook* (pp. 917–922).
[2] Ever.

ch. ends p. 43

"November 8th, 1914.

"Dearest of Friends:
"I'm so glad you are up and about once again. I've been very lonesome, *mon ami*, and being somewhat sympathetic — by nature perhaps—or shall I say to be *mutual?* — well, anyway, I have been sick, also, ever since I last saw you. But so soon as I find you up and around I, too, immediately get better. Now what is it — mutuality? or — well, I think I know what it is, but I also think I'd better wait for some time yet before I express even to myself what I feel it is. Don't you think so, too? But never mind, *mon ami*, the purest gems are not always found on the surface. A little patient work for awhile yet and you may perhaps find many that will shine with brilliancy. God never allowed a man to work as hard as you have, and are still doing, without giving him a fitting reward, both here and elsewhere. Just think of how your dearest mother feels when she looks down through the windows of Heaven and sees all the good her boy is doing for other mothers' sons. And what happy times those mothers must spend together with her in the center of the circle as they chat together and go over all the good you are doing. Now I shall not tire you any more, *cher ami*.[3] Just a word more. Keep cheerful, and get well and strong as soon as you can. Now goodnight, dearest of friends. God bless and keep you is the prayer of one who shall be most sincerely yours as long as you wish it so. Love from Billy, George, and everybody."

Once when Mr. Osborne was ill, Blackie sent him a charming little photograph of clouds and sea, with the following message written on the back:

[3] Translated from French: dear friend.

"Dearest Friend:

"This cloud effect is so beautiful I thought perhaps you would enjoy it. God set this scene away out in the Southland, then told the photographer to make a picture from it, then he asked a dear friend to purchase it and forward it to me. It has made me happy — in turn I pass it on to you, hoping you will also be pleased."

At times Blackie was very much depressed. The disease was making rapid progress and his strength was failing. He realized this and would speak sadly of his approaching end for he wanted to live keenly. He wanted the chance to make good, to help the cause for which his beloved friend was laboring so indefatigably. He sent the following original verse to Mr. Osborne after one of these periods of melancholy:

"God of love, most peerless Lord of all
Be loving, kind, forgive us when we fall;
With tender patience guide our wandering feet,
You are our hope, our rest, our solace sweet.
Till all this strife below is o'er and passed,
We ask your loving aid in first and last,
Meet us at Heaven's gate when this life's work is done,
Again we ask in Mary's name and that of Thy dear Son!"

In the summer of 1914 Mr. Osborne invited the Hon. E. Kent Hubbard, of Middletown, Conn., director of the Connecticut Reformatory at Cheshire, to visit Auburn prison. Mr. Hubbard became a warm friend to many of the prisoners — especially to Blackie, in whom he was immediately interested. That visit was the initial cause of a branch of the Mutual Welfare League being established at Cheshire. The following extracts are taken from some of Blackie's letters to Mr. Hubbard:

"September 12th, 1914.

"Dear Friend:

"Have you thought e'er this that I have forgotten you? No, no, Mr. Hubbard, not so. To be frank, I have been writing all my spare letters to Donald Lowrie. He has been sick and I felt that he would be pleased to hear from me. You know Donald and I are fast friends and having lived so long in California myself, why — well, I guess I can cover it all by saying that my heart often rambles back there. Don will be here next November. He and Mr. Osborne are good friends and work together in this humane uplift work. I wish you could meet him when he comes East but perhaps you may. I think I remember your saying you were going to get his book — *My Life in Prison*. He is a grand fellow and when I say that it is a tie between him and Mr. Osborne — the love I have for both, I mean — why then you will have some conception as to how much I think of him — for you already know how Mr. Osborne has walked right into my heart — all of our hearts here, I may add. Well, we are doing fine here. Everything is running in apple-pie order[4] — New England apple pie — you know the kind I mean, the large-hearted, thick slices, eh? The good old motherly kind. Well, that's the way things are turning out here. We have now a branch of the M. W. L. out in town. One of our boys went home and Mr. Osborne suggested we start this branch and have a man out there as secretary. The executive committee can now recommend outgoing parole men to him. He finds employment and extends a helping hand to all we deem worthy. How long do you suppose it will be before we have a branch of this kind in every city in the State? Not so very, eh?

[4] In perfect organized order.

when the people begin to see that we are determined to 'Do Good and Make Good.' Our motto as you already know. And for good measure I shall add what you said at our meeting in the warden's office — '*Stay good.*' We will, Mr. Hubbard, and we all sincerely hope that you will have the same success with your boys there, as Mr. Osborne has had with us here. Go right to it, dear friend. *You can* win the confidence of the fellows. I *know* it. You won everyone here. Every man you met here has talked — and is still talking — of you. I do not wish to flatter you, Mr. Hubbard, but I am going to be frank. You have made a lasting impression with the boys here. Every time your name is mentioned someone will say, 'That's a square guy.' Another will say 'He sure is; he's an ace.' And I have often heard them say, 'He's right, all the way.' I tell you these remarks prove that you can win out there just as you have here. It's not flattery as I said but honest stuff. I shall have to close now, but will write again, if you wish. Best regards and most sincere wishes from all.

"P. S. Billy Duffy says, 'Tell him to hurry up and come to see us.' I join him in sending regards to your boys. The cigars were splendid. Thanks, ever so much."

✳

"November 8th, 1914.

"Have you thought I am going to forget you? No, no, *mon ami*. It is not that, but you see I have had so many letters to answer and my writing privilege has been limited to one letter each week. Now, however, we can write as often as we have the necessary funds to pay postage. So tonight I am making up for lost

ch. ends p. 43

time. Could you only get a peep into my niche in the wall, you would think I was correspondence clerk for some large manufacturing firm. I'm head over heels in letters. Well, it seems good to be able to write to those whom I consider my friends, and you I think of always as one of my warmest. Mr. Osborne dropped in this P.M. to shake hands and let us know he is up and about once more. He has been sick for a few days. Won't you drop him a line of cheer? Do, please. Billy Duffy is writing to you. I wish you could see him. He looks like a quarterback, and I think he would make a star player, don't you, too? Donald Lowrie is to start east on the 10th or 15th inst.[5] Now get your board of directors together and come on *here*. We will give you and them all the whys and wherefores and *convince* you all that this work is right. Tell your little boy that when I said you are a *square guy*, that I *do* know *you*. And that I am only one out of many here who think the same. I had a BIG talk with a fellow today. Sent him away converted. We can do the same with the most stubborn folks you have in good old Connecticut. Just let us try, that's all we ask Well, I will close now by promising to answer more promptly now that I can, so don't fail to write. Your letters always will be royally welcomed. Best regards and wishes from all the boys."

*

"December 6th, 1914.

"Your letters arrived safely. Also the copies of *The Chronicle*. You have some very bright boys over there, Mr. Hubbard, and I know the movement will be a success. The bylaws you framed were gone over very

[5] Abbreviation of instant, which in this context means: of the current month.

carefully by Mr. Osborne and a few of us fellows here, and everything is O.K., with a couple of exceptions. These, if you will permit, we can talk over when you come to us on the 12th inst. Remember now, the 12th. Mr. Osborne will be here also, and — well, you just *must* be here. I suppose you have been following the newspapers closely lately. Poor 'Tom Brown' comes in for his share of criticism, eh? Well, it doesn't bother him one little bit. Just simply spurs him on. He sure is one grand man, and believe me, old Sing Sing will soon be clean enough to live in. We got a few messages down ahead of him. No matter how, of course — but we made sure that the best fellows there would rally to his call, and last night a very cheering letter came, which says, 'The boys are with me.' That's nice, eh? Now you can and will be the 'Tom Brown' of Connecticut. Just keep up that brave heart of yours and you will win to the front with colors flying. It's an uphill fight, but the best battles ever won were fought bravely for. Stand shoulder to shoulder with your boys and you will just have to win out in the end. I wish I could be there to help you, for I'm surely in love with the work. We expect Donald Lowrie any time now. Shall I get you in touch with him when he arrives? One of the lady workers in New York asked me to send him to her when he comes. They are planning some big work and want him to do some speaking. Well, I'll not tire you any more tonight. We will have a long talk when you get here on the 12th. Well, goodnight. Best wishes for you and your loved ones. Tell your boys, I say to keep it up."

✳

"December 21st, 1914.

"Just a few lines tonight as it's now 10:30 and I must retire to my Ostermoor.[6] I received your last letter safely, also the paper with the article marked. It's great, eh? We sure won't quit now, will we? I suppose that you have already heard that you, Mr. Elton, and the Judge are now honorary members. That means that you are 'Tom Brown of Connecticut' and the Judge and Mr. Elton are pals who will stand by you till the cows come home.

"Your namesake, Elbert Hubbard, spoke here a few nights ago. He is splendid and a strong supporter of the M. W. L. I was introduced to him and like him very much. I see in the paper that you have been down to see our 'Tom Brown' again. That's right, Tom; see as much of our Tom as you can. And say! don't fail to bring Mr. Garvin here when next you come. Well, everyone here sends best regards and all wish you and the rest a very happy Christmas. Also a bright and peaceful New Year. Write when you have time. Tell the others to do so also. Goodnight, Tom.

"Yours to a crisp."

✱

On Labor Day, 1914, the then District Attorney Whitman spoke to the prisoners in the yard at Auburn after the athletic contest. His address made a deep impression — especially upon Blackie, who felt moved to express his appreciation

[6] Blackie demonstrating his keen sense of humor as Ostermoor & Co. has been a luxury mattress manufacturer since 1853.

that evening in the following letter, which was sent to
Mr. Whitman:

"September, 1914.

"Dear Sir:

"Having heard that you were going to address us
inmates here today I made it a special point to be
where I could see your face, and hear every word.
I stood directly underneath you all the while you were
speaking. And I am pleased very much — as I assure
you — to state that the look in your eyes was as sincere
as the ring in your voice. Now, Mr. Whitman, I will
be frank with you. When the news came to us men
here in this world, *intra muras*,[7] that you were in
the race for Governor, we — that is, a number of us
— felt depressed — knowing that the continuance of
our Welfare League depended in a large measure on
the man our State sends to Albany next Fall. We, of
course — naturally, may I add? — felt that we wanted
a man who would be with us, and we felt that you
might not be that man. But now — well, I guess if
you could be elected from here you would win in a
walk. You stood up there on those old steps — they are
nearly a century old, I'm told — and faced a crowd
of convicted men. You heard their hearty cheers for
you, and must have sensed that warm heart-glow
that comes to one when he feels he is in right. Your
presence here and your address delivered to fourteen
hundred convicted men by a district attorney shows
you to be a man of iron nerve. I think I am safe in
saying that you are the only district attorney in this
State, or any other for that matter, who was so royally
received, and the cheers that went up for you from
these good, warm-hearted fellows, were — believe me,

[7] Translated from Latin: within the walls.

honest. Mr. Whitman, so sure am I that Mr. Osborne and his associates have at last found the much sought for prison reform that I would stake my life on the issue. The psychological moment has arrived. Should we eliminate all the other good things done since this great uplift movement began and simply take your reception here today as an illustration, I feel confident you would join me in saying that that alone was a grand — a big thing. When a district attorney who is known as a very strict preserver of society's welfare, and who has sent many of these men here in performance of his duties to society, can get up and address that same body of men and receive the hearty applause you did, why nothing on earth can stop even the most skeptical from saying the movement must be right. What Mr. Osborne and the League have done for me alone would take a volume to tell. But from being one of New York's worst prisoners — under the old system — I am now under this new humane one, striving to be one of the best and shall strive honestly to do so — to keep it up. We have a little movement on here now which we hope to make into a large one before long, i.e., we have adopted the indefinite sentence[8] and started a parole board of our own. When an inmate transgresses against any of the prison rules he is taken in hand by a Grievance Committee. If convicted he stays in his cell while the other members in good standing are allowed the privileges. After some time has expired the Committee Board interviews the man. If they think him fit to be reinstated they recommend him to the Executive Committee who may or may not parole him. The Executive Committee uses pretty fair judgment and so far the indefinite sentence and parole system have been

[8] Rather than an exact number, indefinite sentencing is a range of years, where inmates showing progress toward rehabilitation receive a sentence closer to the minimum term.

a success. Another big movement is being tried out in town. Men eligible for parole by the State Board are sometimes handicapped by not having situations. Of course it is necessary for a man to have employment before the State Board can parole him. Our league is represented outside by a competent man. When a man in here comes to the Executive Committee and states he cannot find employment the Committee after very careful examination into the applicant's case, recommend him if they deem him worthy, to the League's secretary out in town. He looks up work for the man, and when it is procured the man is paroled by the State Parole Board if they in turn think it advisable to consider the recommendation sent to them by the inmate Executive Committee. Now, just one more item. I think it is too important to let go by. Since Mr. Osborne started this good work we have not had *one single case of suicide.* Under the old system I'm told the average deaths of that kind were from six to eight in a year. Now, Mr. Whitman, in all fairness may I ask, is not that alone about the most wonderfully humane thing you have heard of in some time? I think Mr. Osborne and the officials should each have a Carnegie life-saving medal,[9] do you not also? Well, I will not tire you altogether so will close by stating that after eleven years of the old way I never even tried to reform, but now my thoughts and actions are all for the best, and I sincerely hope this good work continues for I, like hundreds of my fellow inmates, do want to 'Do Good and Make Good.'"

---

[9] The Carnegie Medal is a bronze medallion three inches in diameter and is awarded to civilians who risk death or serious physical injury to an extraordinary degree saving or attempting to save the lives of others.

6
Blackie and His "Mother"

One Sunday morning, in October, as Blackie drew aside the curtains on the chapel platform in preparation for the service, he looked out over the crowd of gray-garbed men, and saw sitting in the visitors' box, someone who seemed to be the ghost of his dead mother. His heart almost ceased to beat as he gazed, for the woman's face was startlingly like his mother's, and brought vividly to his mind all the dear days of his childhood, and the sacred associations of home. It had been twelve years since he had talked with any woman, and while he longed to unburden his heart to some understanding mother, yet he also shrank from doing so. He sent word to her by one of his pals that he would like to talk with her, but twice when she went to the prison to see him, he refused the interview. Finally, on her third visit she sent him a message to the effect that she "intended staying there until she saw him if she had to stay ten days!" Then she went to the warden's office and waited. In a few minutes he came, and they talked for over an hour. That was the beginning of a wonderful friendship — a friendship which filled his remaining days with infinite peace and affection. As they parted that autumn afternoon — for the woman was obliged to return to New York — Blackie said to her hesitatingly, "May I ask a very great favor of you? It would mean everything to me, and could not possibly harm you, for I have not long to live — and it is only because of this that I ask it — may I write to you as if you were my mother? And may I think of you and call you that?" With dim eyes she told him how happy she would be to have him do so, that she understood how he felt, for she had a grown son of her own, and that she would try in every way possible to live up to the trust and confidence he placed in her. Then began a remarkable correspondence. The floodgates of an intense nature were flung wide, and the rush of long pent up emotions swept away the years of reserve, and brought to light all the concealed treasures of a deeply sensitive, poetic soul. Mr. Osborne realized that he had struck gold when he first met that forceful character with all its exterior roughness — gold that hitherto no one else had taken the trouble to mine, but which he felt would reveal untold riches.

Permission to use extracts from Blackie's correspondence with his new "mother" has been granted, for it is felt that in no other way could such a revelation of one side of his real self be given. The following letter is the first that he sent to her; in it he refers to Mr. Osborne as his "Viking":

"October 24th, 1914.

"Dearest Friend:
"Shall you mind so very much if I call you that? I haven't many friends, you see, and tonight I feel as though I would like to have one who I feel understands. This has been a beautiful day. One full of glorious sunshine. The sky was dappled with little fleecy cloudlets, gold-lined by the sun's bright rays. The night I presume is splendid also, though I cannot see very much of it, but as I gazed awhile ago through

my window away out to where I know is the ocean of stars, I allowed myself a little diversion from this dull monotony by painting a few mental pictures. I seemed to see a phantom ship laden deeply with promises of hope. At her helm was a sturdy Norseman. By his side stood — a woman — a mother, whose face was so sweet and kind that I knew instinctively God alone had designed it. I gazed intently into the face of the man at the wheel and recognized — my Viking — he seems to be directing the ship's course straight toward me. The woman's face is not yet clear to me, but I feel I shall know her some day, and that all then will be right — for as I allowed my gaze to wander still higher I seemed to see my own dearest mother looking down through one of the windows of Heaven — and she was smiling a sweet approval. Quite a dreamer, you will say. True. And I love to dream. You will perhaps now get a faint conception of how I used to laugh at the darkness and solitude of that twenty months of blackness when I did not have even a single ray of sunshine to gaze upon. Some day I may tell you about the little cricket who often came to cheer me with its homelike little song, but I shall not tire you any more tonight. I am wondering though if I shall ever come to really know that sweet mother I saw tonight on 'The Ship of My Dreams.' *Au revoir*,[1] dearest of friends."

✳

"My dearest Friend:

"Your kind letter arrived safely. It is indeed nice for me to know that you have confidence in me — so nice that at times I find myself eagerly yearning to be worth this faith and trust you so kindly place in me

---

[1] Translated from French: Goodbye.

ch. ends p. 52

— an utter stranger. Dreaming again, you see. Strange thoughts for a bad man to have, you will say. Yes, I admit it. But strange thoughts do sometimes come to one who is so much alone — but as Burroughs[2] says:

> "What matter if I stand alone?
> I wait with joy the coming years;
> My heart *shall* reap where it hath sown
> And garner up its fruit of tears.'

"Shall I give you the first four lines also?

> "Asleep, awake, by night or day
> The friends I seek are seeking me.
> No wind can drive my bark astray
> Nor change the tide of destiny.'[3]

"Another gem from memory's jewel casket. I have many such and they are very comforting at times. The poem by Mr. Le Gallienne is splendid.[4] I shall memorize it also. Yes, I have read Wilde's 'Reading Gaol' and have *felt* all he says in it.[5] When I can talk to you I will tell you something that I know will make you happy. I've seen the face of the lady on the 'Ship of My Dreams'!"[6]

---

[2] John Burroughs (1837–1921) was an American naturalist and nature essayist, active in the conservation movement in the United States.

[3] Stanzas three and four (in reverse order) of Burroughs' poem "Waiting."

[4] Richard Le Gallienne (1866–1947) was an English author and poet.

[5] *The Ballad of Reading Gaol* is a poem by Oscar Wilde (1854–1900), written in exile after his release on May 19, 1897, from Reading Gaol (a former prison located in Reading, Berkshire, England; in operation from 1844 to 2014). Wilde had been incarcerated in Reading after being convicted of "gross indecency" with other men in 1895 and sentenced to two years of hard labor.

[6] Likely a reference to the 1912 song "Ship of My Dreams" with words by English lyricist Arthur J. Lamb (1870–1928) and music by American composer Alfred Solman (1868–1937).

Blackie addressed his new friend as "mother" for the first time in the following letter. He had held back because he wanted to feel *sure* that he could live up to a "mother's" confidence in him. But he had seen the lady on the "Ship of Dreams" and it was all right:

"November, 1914.

"Dearest Mother:

"What sweet memories come to me as I write that dear name — 'Mother'! How many times have I conjured up her sweet face and had little imaginary chats with her, since I first caught a glimpse of the only woman who looks so much like her — only God and myself know. Forgive me for holding back so long, I wanted you — God knows I did — and do, but I was afraid — afraid for both you and myself. Not that I doubted you for one second. No! No! not that. But afraid that I might perhaps bring into your life some sorrow if I proved unworthy, and afraid of myself, when I thought perhaps something might happen which would break our sacred covenant. But something happened a short while ago which makes me think that I still retain a few of mother's teachings. And now, will you grant me what my heart has been yearning for, for years? Will you let me try to go back to my Yesterdays? And will you go hand in hand with me, as I try to cross the bridge from Then to Now? I want to be good. I'm weary — sick and weary of the old life. I want to come out into the sunshine once again, and get out of the shadows. I know I've got to start all over again. I've got to get back to *Her*, and I want your motherly help to do it.

"Your letter received, and I am very happy. If I can only stay on this side of the bridge now, perhaps you will be able to make something of me some day. I hope

ch. ends p. 52

so, for really I am tired and would like to come over and have a nice rest. Don Lowrie has made good, so has Ed. Morrell[7] — read Morrell's story in Lowrie's book.[8] Ed's life and mine both outside and in, have been similar, so much so that you could look upon them as almost one. Ed. is now out, pardoned — and when last I heard of him, he was doing splendid work for the boys inside. I'd give a good deal to work shoulder to shoulder with Don and Ed. "I'm so sorry for all those poor people in the breadline you write of. I wish I could help in some way. One poor fellow in here was saving coupons to get his little baby a Christmas present. He was short forty, but he got them O.K.

"I suppose you have noticed that account of me in the papers. It's rather hard, and perhaps unfair, now that I am trying hard to forget the past. But it's *all right anyway* — so once again 'nuff said![9] Thank you for your promise to help me through the coming year. I may need your motherly love if I have to go to Sing Sing for an operation. Gee! I wonder when I shall ever get a few moments' rest! All this constant pain is hell! Please excuse my French. You see now, do you not, that I have a retentive memory? What's that? Well, Sing Sing is hell — or I should say *was*. But with my 'Tom Brown,' you, Donald Lowrie, and all our other friends, the flames will not scorch so badly anymore.

"Everyone here is in splendid trim. My old pal is battling constantly, and of course we shall always do our little part to help him. I hope you received

---

[7] Edward Morrell (1868–1946) was a member of the Evans and Sontag gang, known for repeatedly robbing the Southern Pacific Railroad in California's San Joaquin Valley in the 1890s, until he surrendered with leader Chris Evans and was sentenced to life imprisonment in Folsom State Prison in 1894. In 1896 he was transferred to San Quentin, where he met Donald Lowrie, and was finally pardoned in 1908. Author Jack London (1876–1916) used Morrell as both inspiration for and as a character in his 1915 novel *The Star Rover*.

[8] Chapters 15–18 of *My Life in Prison* (1912) by Donald Lowrie.

[9] An informal way of saying "enough said."

my Christmas letter. This is for the New Year — and I hope the coming year will be very, very happy — full of peace, joy, and success.

"They say I'm going blind. Won't you send me a photograph? I want to see you many times before the dark comes!"

The desired photograph soon arrived — a picture of the friend whom he called his new "mother" and her little ten year old daughter, who was very greatly interested in Blackie, and who used to write to him calling him "Brother Blackie." One of Blackie's most winning traits was his intense love for children and animals. The following letter to the little girl is a charming illustration:

"Dearest Pet Sister:

"Your beautiful letter received just when I needed it most. You see, dearie, I love little sisters, and you are so sweet and so good that your letter brought ever so much comfort. How did you know I was so fond of pets? Always, all through my life, I have had a pet of some kind. I wish you could have seen the pretty little canary bird I had at Auburn. It was such a loving little creature. I used to open the cage door and let it fly wherever it wanted to, and when it grew tired of flying, it would always come back. I would hold my hand out, and it would light on my finger, and I'd have a seed between my teeth. You ought to have seen how carefully it would reach over and take the seed with its little bill. That was a bird-kiss, wasn't it? I loved that little bird, and missed it very much when it was gone. You see I gave it to little Pauline, Billy's little baby. She had a nice puppy, too. I'm going to see if I can't get a singing bird for my little sister. Wouldn't you like it? You see, dear, I love you already. Mother has told me what a good big brave girl her little woman is, and I just

ch. ends next p.

love brave girls! Continue to be brave, and some day you will be a good, good woman like mother, working for the Cause.

"God bless and protect you my little sister!

"Lovingly your brother,
"BLACKIE."

7

Blackie's Release

On December 31, 1914, Blackie was transferred to Sing Sing prison at Warden Osborne's request. He was so ill that it was thought best to have a throat specialist examine him. He was placed in the hospital at first, but upon examination it was found that the disease had advanced beyond help, and that he had only a few months to live. Mr. Osborne then had him removed to a little room on the third floor of his own house, where he was in charge of a nurse and made as comfortable as possible. Here he was allowed to see his friends, and his new "mother" had the privilege of making frequent visits, which were a great joy to him. That little room under the eaves at Sing Sing was a center of interest in the prison. Members of the Golden Rule Brotherhood,[1] and later of the Mutual Welfare League would come there to consult with that keen mind on important questions, and from that white bed of pain went out many messages of cheer and consolation to others in trouble. During the first month at Sing Sing Blackie was able to walk slowly about the yard

[1] Sing Sing's system of prison self-government that proved lacking and was ultimately replaced by the M.W.L. after Osborne became warden.

or to sit for an hour or two on the piazza in the sunshine, but the weakness gained upon him rapidly, and soon he was unable to leave his bed. It was after one of these "hikes," as he called them, that the following letter was written:

"Your beautiful letter reached me safely, and God bless you! You are a mother indeed. I had been a little tired — or lazy, perhaps, and was lying in bed when your letter came, and believe me, I got right up after reading your brave words; and this afternoon I went into the yard and enjoyed an hour of beautiful sunshine. O, how I shall enjoy the bracing air and sunlight when I grow a little stronger, and more accustomed to the change! You see being housed is rather annoying to me. I do not think I shall ever know what it means to forget; as I lie here my thoughts go roaming away out into God's country, far, far from the glamour and turmoil of the cities; out into the open spots where one can throw back his head and drink deeply of God's life-giving air as it flows direct from His throne. Someday, perhaps, I can tell you of Dan, my pony, and a little something of our madcap gallops clean up into the foothills. Dan was my only pal in those days, and, believe me, we grew to know each other wonderfully well. If I drew him down into a walk to let him rest, he would telegraph up to me through the bridle rein when he had rested sufficiently, then away we would go on another mad dash. It was great! and I can't forget. I'm getting good attention here. Everyone tries his best to help in some way, but I'm not used to all this hot-house stuff. I would get well quicker if I were only out roughing it. But I'm going to win with flying colors yet! You know I cannot part from you now. You are so brave, so hopeful and so kind that I'm really ashamed to be sick."

Shortly after this Blackie was made supremely happy by being elected an honorary member of the Mutual Welfare League at Auburn prison, and in receiving the silver button. It was given to him without one dissenting vote, of which fact he was very proud. He described his happiness in this letter:

"O, how happy your boy is tonight! Just think! 'Tom Brown' is here with me, and has just pinned a silver button on my breast, given to me by the Auburn delegates for — as they say — 'Invaluable good work for our M.W.L.' I don't deserve all this love, but it is very delightful nevertheless, and I know you will be happy, and I can't wait another second, so I'm bolstered up here as 'snug as a bug in a rug,' writing you. There are only two such buttons in all these places, one for Jack Murphy for starting the League, and one to your boy for — well, 'nuff said! But I'm the happiest man in the known world — honest I am — and 'Tom Brown' says *I'm to go home!* O, God is good! I know it now. You cannot say now that my dreams shall ever go astray, can you 'mother'? Every dream I have woven shall be beautifully triumphant, and I know I shall make your heart beat with gladness, when you begin to hear people talk of, and point to me with pride. I feel that I have it in me to go to any height, and I'm so happy! Now rest so that you can come up soon well and strong to share in my joy. You see I must settle down all the more now, and be ever so good, all in honor of the Cause and my precious button. I wish you could see all the letters brought to me by 'Tom Brown' from the boys at Auburn. It's good to be loved, isn't it?"

A friend who was visiting Blackie one day, said she had an address to make on prison reform, and asked his advice about it. Immediately he became interested, for it was the subject nearest his heart. His eyes flashed with enthusiasm as he answered —

"Just talk like the warden does. Tell them about the cold damp cell block, wherein sick men have to huddle, and also about the cent and a half a day wages; about the wives and babies who suffer more than we do. Of the misery it brings to the man inside when he knows his kiddies and wife are perhaps without a fire on cold nights, and with perhaps not even bread in the larder for breakfast in the morning. Tell them that the State is making criminals and anarchists out of the children, street-walkers out of the poor wives who are forced to do it rather than see their little brood starve and separated from them. Tell them of the hardened criminals you have seen, who, under the old system of cruelty, could not even be forced into a moan by all the torture, but whose eyes now light with love and reverence when the warden speaks to them. Tell them of the trust placed in the man whom the old administration called 'the bad man.' Tell them that that same brand of men is now being trusted, and up to date not one has betrayed the trust. O, you know millions of things to tell them, and every word will be the truth. You have seen them, you have heard the men talk, you have seen the look in their eyes, you have had the personal experience. Prison reform may be a dream, but it is a dream that is coming true, and *soon*. A little firm determination, patience, perseverance, and a cheerful heart and the whole world will leap to your will!"

The evening of February 16th, 1915, stands out with an especial radiance in the minds of those privileged to be present when Blackie received his pardon.[2] He had been very ill for days, and it was feared that the end was near,

[2] At right is the request for pardon signed by Governor Charles Whitman.

Albany, *Feb. 16, 1915*

The Secretary of State is requested to make out a

Pardon

~~Restoration to the Rights of Citizenship~~ for

John Murphy

who was convicted in the Counties of { *Schoharie* *Clinton* }

of the crimes of { *murder 2nd degree* and *Assault* }

and sentenced { *April, 1903* and *May, 1912* }

to { *Life* and *10 years* }

imprisonment in the *Sing Sing Prison*

~~and to pay a fine of $~~

Charles S. Whitman

so early on the morning of the 16th, Donald Lowrie was dispatched to Albany to bring back the promised pardon from the Governor. He returned about seven o'clock in the evening bearing the precious document, and Blackie knew of his return, but he steadfastly refused to receive the pardon until his beloved warden, who was lecturing in New York, could be there.[3] Finally, well toward midnight, the familiar sound of the motor was heard, and at last Mr. Osborne appeared with the significant white paper in his hand. With his characteristic thoughtfulness, he did not give it direct to Blackie, but handed it instead to Billy Duffy — Blackie's closest pal, and the "whitest friend a man ever had," as Blackie once said of him — and Billy sat on the side of the bed and read aloud in a voice that broke in spite of all his efforts at self-control, the words that made Blackie a free man! One prisoner giving a pardon to another! Had such a thing ever happened before? Truly this was the "new system." Blackie's new "mother" knelt beside him with his hand in hers, and a hushed group of loyal pals, stood wet-eyed in the doorway. Blackie's voice failed him, but his great eyes shone with an eloquence far beyond words.

The next day came telegrams and letters filled with congratulations. Messages glowing with sincere love and friendship, some of which were overwhelming in their deep emotion. One letter in particular was almost heartbreaking in its pathetic joy; it was from a boy of nineteen in the death-house at Auburn, saying how glad he was for Blackie's good fortune, and bidding him "cheer up"! This boy has since been electrocuted.

One of the last letters Blackie was able to write to his new "mother" was sent a few days after this — a letter that reveals the deep soul of the man.

[3] Interestingly, Lowrie recounts a different version of this same event in the excerpt from his book *Back in Prison—Why?*, which we have included later in this book.

"Well, 'mother' dear, this has been a very busy day
for me. Visits all day long — publishers, politicians, and
ladies! I'm at home now to all who are kind enough to
call. 'O. K. Bill' was the first this morning. He rushes
in with that big broad-gauge smile of his, and the room
is immediately filled with beautiful sunshine. I wish
society had about one man in every ten like Bill; he
would easily round the other nine into wearing the
right glasses, through which to gaze upon this dusty
old world of ours. When are you coming again? I'm
safe from myself and everything else when I have you
in mind. I cannot do any harm when you are with me.
You say I do not realize what a wonderful help *I* am to
you. Now please reverse that, won't you? Instead of me
being a help to you, you have been the one to whom
my thoughts have flown when perplexed and almost
despondent. You will never know how many times
I have had to conjure up your face to help me fight
some battles which I confess to you were at times
heartbreaking. I wonder if you can get the slightest
inkling of how much alone I was until you came to
me. True, I had many loyal friends, but I mean alone
without mother and my little sister. You came like a
thunderbolt from a clear sky that Sunday, and you just
took me by storm. Do you remember how I tried to
fight against letting you into my heart? How I refused
to go upon the steps and talk with you when you sent
for me? Had you been like any other woman you would
have allowed the matter to drop then and there, and
I would have won my battle, but lost the most loyal
and truest of friends. But you persisted and won, did
you not? I simply gave up my sword to the bravest
general in this big army of the universe. I admire your
gameness, and I surrendered to my general in all sincerity. There are many loyal hearts under these suits
of gray, and they love my 'mother.' That repays me

ch. ends p. 63

for all the lonesome past. To those who have suffered, sometimes there comes a time when one can say, "I, too, am happy!' It is not so easy for anyone to gain the confidence of men in prison. They have been imposed upon so many times, that in time they get to be rather skeptical, and shy away from any advances. But you took us all by storm. Mr. Osborne won the love of all. Next to him you are the only one who really lives in our hearts. Well, it's just as I've heard it often remarked — 'She's on the level!' and that goes all the way with us."

Over twenty years ago Blackie was sent to the Reformatory at Joliet, Illinois — at that time said to be one of the worst spots of human brutality on the map — and recently in that sickroom under the warden's roof at Sing Sing occurred one of the most dramatic incidents in Blackie's entire career. Mr. Osborne brought to his bedside the former warden of Joliet — the warden who first inflicted physical torture upon him — and such torture! He was put in the straitjacket for days at a stretch, and every time the guard came near him the lacings would be drawn tighter. He was suspended by steel handcuffs on his wrists so that his toes just touched the floor, and left in that position for hours. Every method of the "old system" was used in the effort to break his spirit — to say nothing of his body! The result of that term in Joliet was that Blackie became an outlaw — one of the bravest and most unscrupulous in the country. But the Joliet warden as well as Blackie had learned his lesson, and on the day that he bent over the wasted frame of the idomitable spirit that he had once tortured cruelly, truce was declared between them, and sincere remorse filled the warden's heart, for the marks of the steel handcuffs were still on Blackie's emaciated wrists. A particularly courageous action of Blackie's in connection with this same warden, occurred at a meeting of the Executive Committee of the League in Auburn at the time of Mr. Hubbard's visit to the prison, Mr. Hubbard was desirous of getting points in regard to the character of the warden who was going to look after the new reformatory in Connecticut. Now it happened that it was the former warden of Joliet, and Blackie was the only man on the Executive Committee who knew him, which fact he stated, thereby admitting that he, Blackie, had done time before, though he had entered Auburn prison as a first-timer. It was the chance that he ran of losing his credits, and of getting in very wrong with the authorities by this admission that showed his courage. It was heroic, and helped a great deal, because he was in possession of facts which were of much service to Mr. Hubbard.

Blackie's words were true. The "sand" was rapidly slipping through his hour glass, and in less than a month after the electrocution, referred to at the beginning of this account, Blackie himself had passed into the great silence. Just about sunrise on March twentieth, 1915, he suddenly raised himself from his pillows, and with a wave of his hand, murmured "More light!" — the words that the dying poet Goethe made immortal[4] — and then quietly ceased to breathe.

His body was cremated at his own request, for he felt strongly the danger of spreading the dread disease by ordinary burial. His ashes were returned to Sing Sing, and on Palm Sunday was held the first funeral service in the history of the prison. No one present that day will ever forget it. Some sixteen hundred men stood bareheaded in the yard, in the brilliant sunshine of a perfect Spring afternoon, as the little funeral procession headed by the prison band playing a dirge, slowly wound its way among the lines of gray men to the chapel. Six members of the League bore the bier,[5] on which rested the ashes, enclosed in an exquisitely inlaid box made by a prisoner. This box was covered by a black

---

[4] Johann Wolfgang von Goethe (1749–1832) was a German poet, playwright, novelist, scientist, statesman, theater director, and critic widely regarded as the greatest and most influential writer in the German language. When he died, Goethe's last words were, according to his doctor, "Mehr licht!" (More light!).

[5] A stand on which a corpse or a coffin containing a corpse is placed before burial.

ch. ends next p.

velvet pall,[6] on which was pinned the delegate badge of the Mutual Welfare League, of which Blackie was so justly proud. A great wreath of myrtle leaves surrounded the little box, and at either end of the bier were sheaves of calla lilies, a flower Blackie especially loved. The services were very simple. After some verses of Scripture, two beautiful sacred songs, and a prayer, Warden Osborne spoke feelingly. "If ever a man had a right to have a grudge against society — to wish to pay back his wrongs to the world — Blackie had it," he said. "But my friends, no one has that right, and no one came to see that point of view more clearly than he did. He bent all the powers of a forceful, remarkable mind toward helping his fellow prisoners — his fellowmen. One of the most characteristic incidents of Blackie's life occurred when the chaplain went in to see him. Blackie did not want any misunderstanding. I hope you don't think that after what I've been and what I've done, that I intend at this last moment to try to 'sneak' into Heaven, he said. But" — continued Mr. Osborne, "no one can 'sneak' into Heaven, and Blackie has gone in by the open gate!"

On Easter Sunday a memorial service was held in the chapel at Auburn prison, a service just as impressive as the one at Sing Sing, and in many ways more so, for it was in Auburn that Blackie was best known and loved. There was no marching through the yard, but as the procession entered the chapel, the band led the singing of "Nearer My God to Thee." The chapel was brave with Spring flowers. There was no note of death there. It was all triumph! A never-to-be-forgotten Easter service. Blackie's spirit lived that day in the hearts of everyone in that crowded hall, as it shall continue to live in the hearts of all who knew the real Blackie. As the little procession left the chapel to bear the earthly remains to their last resting place in Fort Hill cemetery, some fourteen hundred prisoners sang "Lead, Kindly Light," and no other music ever seemed quite so thrilling to those who vainly

---

[6] A cloth cover spread over a coffin, bier, or tomb.

tried to join in, for a great resurrection light was flooding the "encircling gloom" of that prison as never before. Blackie's prayer was indeed answered. He had "*counted*."

"More light!" he cried, and then God drew away
Life's threadbare curtain and he entered light.
At last the sun rose after starless night;
Out of long darkness dawned the golden day.
His debt is paid — let all the scoffers say
Whate'er they please, for in a desperate fight
He conquered wrong with the white sword of right
Though his bruised body fell amid the fray.

More light he gave to us who loved him well,
Light for our hearts so blind to others' woe,
Because he lived we are made strong to tell
How men can overcome. Grieving we know
His deepest need was to be understood,
That he might prove these words —
  "Do good: Make good."

The New Penology
(An Excerpt)

As printed in
Society and Prisons (1916)
by
Thomas Mott Osborne

Perhaps the most remarkable instance of the transforming power of the League lies in the story of Canada Blackie. That has been told in full elsewhere,[1] but its main points will bear retelling.

Blackie was a dark-eyed and black-haired white man, born in Canada. The death of his dearly-loved mother and the severity of an unsympathetic father were the causes of his leaving home. Before the age of twenty he was in state prison, after having been circus performer, cow-boy, train bandit, and Heaven knows what beside. He once told me that he had never stolen from one that could not afford to lose the money, and seemed to think that it was to his credit that his robberies were confined to banks, postoffices and express companies. There is more than a touch of Robin Hood in many of our criminals.

In various prisons Blackie was the victim of the usual brutalities which the old system has meted out to vigorous and high-tempered youth. Remember that it was the belief even of the conscientious supporters of the old system that the spirit of prisoners must be broken; and when successive wardens tried and failed to break the

[1] See "The Story of Canada Blackie," by Anna F. L. Field — published by E. P. Dutton & Co.

The New Penology

Perhaps the most remarkable instance of the transforming power of the League lies in the story of Canada Blackie. That has been told in full elsewhere, but its main points will bear retelling.

Blackie was a dark-eyed and black-haired white man, born in Canada. The death of his dearly-loved mother and the severity of an unsympathetic father were the causes of his leaving home. Before the age of twenty he was in state prison, after having been circus performer, cowboy, train bandit, and Heaven knows what beside. He once told me that he had never stolen from one that could not afford to lose the money, and seemed to think that it was to his credit that his robberies were confined to banks, post offices, and express companies. There is more than a touch of Robin Hood in many of our criminals.

In various prisons Blackie was the victim of the usual brutalities which the old system has meted out to vigorous and high-tempered youth. Remember that it was the belief even of the conscientious supporters of the old system that the spirit of prisoners must be broken; and when successive wardes tried and failed to break the indomitable spirit, which God had placed in this man, they called him "an incorrigible" and treated him with still greater brutality.

In the year 1903 there was a bank robbery at Cobleskill, Schoharie County, N.Y., and a watchman was killed. Exactly how much Blackie had to do with it we are not likely to know now; for after his arrest, true to "the ethics of his profession," he refused to talk. Two men went to death in the electric chair; Blackie and another were sent to Clinton prison with life sentences. In New York State a man sentenced to "life" is eligible for parole at the end of twenty years; and Blackie started off bravely and uncomplainingly to do his new bit. For seven years he had a perfect record; then something happened. Either the doctor was to blame for an inconsiderate lack of tact, or else Blackie's nerves had worn thin through long confinement — as nerves have a habit of doing; at any rate, the result was the same; impatience, insolence, punishment, bad conduct, and more punishment. Months of solitary confinement in a dark cell made the man desperate. With three others there was a mad attempt at escape; before they were overpowered Blackie had shot a guard through the shoulder with a pistol he had manufactured out of a piece of gas pipe, getting the explosive by scraping the sides of matchboxes. For this act he was placed on trial before the county court and given an additional ten years. He was then taken back to prison and put in the dark cell again.

In all he was in the dark cell for one year and eight months; with no bed or blankets, sleeping on the bare stone floor, winter and summer, and keeping his reason only by inventing games; thinking over all the poetry he had learned as a child and bringing it back to his memory line by line; tearing the buttons off his shirt and then standing at one end of the cell and throwing the buttons over his shoulder; if he found all the buttons before he finished adding up to a certain number, it counted one for him — if not, it counted one for the buttons.

At the end of the twenty months Blackie came out of the dark cell blind in one eye, and ill with the tuberculosis which eventually brought his death.

He came out of the dark cell — but only to be shut in solitary confinement in a light cell. For three years he was thus "in isolation," supposed to communicate with no man but the jailer; nevertheless he managed to get word to those outside and the authorities heard of dynamite hidden somewhere about the prison yard. When I once asked Blackie about this, he turned upon me almost fiercely. "It was there, all right," he said; "I intended to blow out the end of the cell-block while the men were away at dinner. Yes," he admitted, "someone might have been killed; but wouldn't you do it, if you were in for life?"

I thought it wise to turn the subject without answering the question.

Blackie was transferred, heavily handcuffed and shackled, to Auburn prison, where he was immediately placed again in solitary confinement. Here he had been for over a year when I made his acquaintance.

A very nervous, broken man it was to whom I was introduced through the bars of his cell-door. I was not aware that it was the wild and dangerous criminal of whom I had heard so much. We shook hands and began conversation. Soon I asked him how long a bit he had. He turned upon me with a curious, inscrutable look. "Life — and ten years." Then seeing the smile which I could not conceal, he added: "It does seem a little superfluous, doesn't it?"

That was the beginning of a remarkably pleasant friendship. Two or three times I had the privilege of sitting with him an hour or so in his cell, talking of prisons and prison reform. I found he had many excellent and practical ideas, — which at my request he reduced to writing for the benefit of the Commission on Prison Reform. He was keenly interested in my week's incarceration; and kept track of all the details of the formation of the Mutual Welfare League, in

ch. ends p. 78

the mysterious way that a clever prisoner apparently always succeeds in doing in spite of the rules. The influence of the new system, as the League developed, penetrated even to the isolation cells and broke down a desperate resolve that Blackie had been cherishing. For many months he had been laying plans for another attempt to escape — a desperate and dangerous chance; but what did life hold for him but his solitary cell, a cot in the hospital, a convict's lonely death-bed and an unknown grave in that saddest of all places — the prison cemetery — "*Twenty-five gallery*" — as they call it in Sing Sing — the highest numbered gallery in the cell-block being Twenty-four.

At Auburn prison Decoration Day, 1914, with its accompanying quarantine for scarlatina,[1] passed as was described in the last lecture — the races and games and long, sunny afternoon in the yard. May 31st brought the granting of the first regular hour of recreation; June 1st continued the custom; and on the next day I received word from the isolation building that Blackie wished to see me. In the afternoon I gained the necessary permission and stood in front of his cell.

"Come in here, I want to say something to you."

For a month or more I knew Blackie had wished to talk with me in private; in fact, he had urged it upon me several times. He had asked me to get permission for him to be taken out front to the Warden's office, where we could be sure, he said, of not being overheard. "You know these walls have ears and eyes too," he whispered; for he was always afraid one of the "screws" was listening down the corridor, just out of sight.

When I mentioned Blackie's request to the Warden, he shook his head — his office was too near the street; and Blackie was held to be the most desperate and dangerous criminal in the state. "Not that I really think he would do anything," said the Warden; "but he might. I wouldn't want

_____
[1] Scarlet fever.

you to run the risk." And, frankly, I was not altogether sorry
that he held that view.

On this occasion the officer let me into the cell; the grated
door was locked and I sat down on the bed. Blackie wasted
no words. "There is something I want you to do for me,"
he said. Then, reaching down to a shelf below his table, he
produced a can of talcum powder, pulled open the cover, dug
with his finger down through the powder and drew forth a
small parcel. From this he proceeded to unwind a cotton rag
and then handed me a rough key. "That fits the door of my
cell," said he; and added with a tinge of pride: "I don't believe
there's another man in prison could have made that key!"

Then from another hiding place he drew forth a short
piece of steel, fashioned into a knife; and as he placed it in
my hand remarked grimly: "I intended to use that." Then
he seated himself in his rocking chair and faced me. "I want
you to give those to the Warden; and tell him that I feel so
deeply what he and you are trying to do for the men in this
prison that I want him to know he need have no further
anxiety about me — *I'm going straight.*"

And from that moment he never flinched.

In considerable excitement I returned to the office, and
to the warden by long-distance telephone I told my tale,
adding: "I want you to give permission for Blackie to come
out into the yard with me tomorrow." He consented; and the
next day, as soon as the prisoners had marched out of the
prison for the hour of recreation I went again to the isolation
cells. Now let Blackie himself continue the story, as he wrote
it to Donald Lowrie later on the same day. By a curious
coincidence Lowrie, the first ex-prisoner to be permitted to
visit Auburn Prison and the first visitor to be shown around
by a prisoner, was brought to Blackie's cell by William Duffy,
the Sergeant-at-Arms of the League, at the exact moment
that Blackie had tried his key and found that it fitted; and all
the time the three men stood conversing, Blackie was using

ch. ends p. 78

his foot to keep the door firmly closed. A striking group in a dramatic situation!

"June 3rd, 1914.

"Dear Friend Don:

"The above is the date of my new birthday. After five years of a living death in solitary, I have been resurrected again — making my second time on earth, as it were. So you see I was right when I said, "A man can come back." This afternoon Mr. Osborne came to my door and as the officer who accompanied him inserted the key to spring the lock, Mr. Osborne said, "Get your coat and cap, old fellow, I want you to come with me and see something worthwhile." Knowing that the men had recently been given the liberty of the yard, I, of course, immediately divined the kindness about to be bestowed. I at first felt inclined to say that I could not accept the invitation, knowing, though, that it was extended in all kindness. My reason for wanting to refuse was because I felt that I would feel too keenly the embarrassment that comes to one when suddenly placed among his fellowmen after so long an absence. Mr. Osborne would not, however, take no for an answer, and kindly insisted that I should put on my coat, he helping me with it, and chatting pleasantly all the time. This I knew was to put me at ease. . . .

"After traversing the corridor of the isolation building, we came to the double-locked doors — two of them — which lead directly into the main prison yard. As we stepped into the pure air, I felt as though I wanted to bite chunks out of it, but the first deep inhale made me so dizzy that I actually believe I would have staggered had I not taken myself into firm control. On rounding the end of the cloth-shop, we came into full view of the most wonderful, as well as beautiful, sight I have ever seen in prison — or outside, either, for that matter. I hardly know how to describe this sight; but picture to yourself, if you possibly can, fourteen hundred men turned loose in a beautiful park. For years previous to this good work now being promoted by Mr. Osborne and the prison officials, these same men whom I now see running in and out among beautiful flower-beds and playing like a troop of innocent boys just out of school, had been harnessed, as it were, to the machines in their respective shops, without even the privilege of saying goodnight or good morning to their nearest neighbor. But what a wonderful change has come to pass! Instead of the prison pallor and haunted look which once predominated, I now notice smiling eyes, and that clean look which exhilarating exercise in the pure air always brings to the face.

"When Mr. Osborne and I reached the lower end of the park, he invited me to stand where we could get a full view of everything. Among the first things I noticed was a ring of the boys formed around something, I could not see what. Mr. Osborne, in answer to my question, said it was a party of Italian lads, waltzing. Just then someone stepped out of the ring, leaving a space through which I could see the boys dancing to their hearts' content.

"Several of the boys are now waiting to greet me. Billy [Duffy] noticing this, turns to chat with Mr. Osborne so as to give them their turn. We are quite a crowd by this time, everyone laughing and joking. Someone suggests that we walk up to the other end of the park. Billy, hearing this, says, "Yes, come on, old man, it will do you good." I glance over to Mr. Osborne. He smilingly nods consent. So away we go, he joining the party, also. On the way up the walk, I shake hands with many of the boys, who come running up to extend a kind greeting. Some birthday, eh,

ch. ends p. 78

Don? All along the line we pass bunches of the fellows, some dancing, others playing stringed instruments, and out on the lawn are hundreds throwing hand ball. Arriving at the upper end of the park, we all go over to lounge on the lawn. I wish I could convey to you the feeling that came to me as I felt the green yielding grass under my feet. I felt as though I wanted to roll right over; and when you stop to consider that I have not had any grass to stretch out on for over twelve years, you can readily understand my feelings.

"After spending a very happy afternoon, the bugle sounded assembly . . . On both sides of the park the men had formed in double columns on the smooth concrete walks. This gives each man a full view of the beautiful flowerbeds and Old Glory floating in her place at the top of the pole. When the men are all in place, there comes a sudden hush, and then from away up on the extreme right-hand corner from where we stand comes the sweet strain of "The Star Spangled Banner," and as the flag dips her "Good Night, Boys" and is slowly lowered, each inmate and officer bares his head in all honor to her colors. The music ceases, and I hear in a soft voice, "All right, Joe," and Joe, an inmate and delegate of the League, just as softly gives his command, "'Bout face." His company turns as one man; and then another soft, "Forward, march," and away they swing into their cell halls in true military style. After watching several companies run in, Mr. Osborne and I start back to where I belong. In doing this we have to pass between two lines of hundreds of men. As we reach about midway, the boys start a handclapping. They all recognize the kindness bestowed upon me, and show him their appreciation in this manner; and to me their hearty, "Goodnight, Jack, cheer up, old man," coming from all down the line, was good to hear. Arriving at my quarters, Mr. Osborne extends his hand

and bids me a pleasant "goodnight," and thus ends my
birthday into a new and I hope a better life. . . .

   "Well, I am tired, so will close and turn in. I hope
I have not tired you also, Don, with all this; but it's my
birthday, old fellow, and I wanted to share it with you."

The day after this red-letter episode I thought it wiser
for Blackie to stay in his cell, lest the excitement prove too
much for him; but the following day he came out, and the
next, and the next. Within a week he was removed to one of
the regular cells in the north wing; and was at once appointed
an assistant sergeant-at-arms of the League. In July he was
elected delegate of his company (the invalid company)
and received the largest number of votes for the executive
committee. His appearance improved wonderfully; his face,
which was almost the color of his gray coat the first day
I took him into the yard, became ruddy and his eyes regained
their peculiar fire. By September he was one of the most
trusted men in Auburn prison, and justly so; for his voice
was always raised on the side of right and common sense.
No man in prison wielded a greater influence and he always
used it to strengthen the League, the essential principles of
which he grasped with the same keen intellectual force which
had formerly made him a bold and determined criminal. All
the great power of the man which had once been employed
in destruction was now engaged in solving interesting constructive problems.

   "I wish I could get out of that back gate," he said to me one
day, as we were returning to the isolation building, before he
was removed to the cell block.

   "Why?" I asked.

   "So that I could walk right around and come into the front
gate. I'd like to show them what this League means."

   To him it meant something high and holy, something
more than life — it meant service. A passionate desire seized
upon him — a desire to aid his fellow men — which, after

ch. ends p. 78

all, was only another expression of his old loyalty to his pals. This dangerous criminal — this wild-beast, fit only to be caged and beaten and broken — according to the old theories, became one of the most potent forces for good in the whole state of New York.

✳

It may be of interest, before drawing to a close, to conclude the story of Canada Blackie. About the time I became warden of Sing Sing it was evident that the temporary physical improvement that had followed Blackie's release from "solitary" had about run its course, and his relentless disease again fastened its grip upon him. Hoping that the less severe winter of the lower Hudson might prove of benefit, he was transferred to Sing Sing; but it was of little or no avail. He soon took to his bed in the hospital, and when it became necessary, because of the nature of his illness, to remove him from there, he was taken to a small room in the upper story of the Warden's house. Here his friends from the outside as well as those from the inside were allowed to visit him; and here on a memorable night in February he received a pardon from the Governor of New York. He was technically a free man; but freedom of mind and soul he had already attained — freedom of body could no longer be granted, even by the Governor.

His loyalty to the League never faltered for a moment. Even on his deathbed, he was constantly planning how he could help to establish more firmly the foundations of the new reform. A talk he had with one young Italian friend, explaining the proper change of attitude of the members of the League toward the prison authorities, will serve as a sample of this. Using the vernacular of the prison, he said: "Look here, kid; it's this way. When you were in stir [prison,] under the old system, you were always on the level with your pals, weren't you? You'd never squeal on them, or do them dirt. But you used to double-cross the warden and put it over on the screws — sure you did — whenever you had a chance. Well, that was all right — under the old system. But now, you see, it's different. Now the warden is your pal; and you must play straight with him; you must be on the level; for listen, kid — you can't play the game both ways."

His keen sense of humor and hatred of all sham and insincerity remained to the end. When the prison chaplain came to pay a call, he was received with perfect courtesy, and there followed a pleasant chat. When the visit was repeated, Blackie felt it was time to have an explanation. "Father," said he, "I am glad to have you come and see me whenever you feel like it; but don't let's have any misunderstanding. As a friend, you are welcome; but I hope you don't think, after what I've been and after all I've done, that I'm going to try and sneak into Heaven through a back door!"

Yet there was in him no lack of faith or deep religious feeling. On the morning of February 26, 1915, just ten days after Blackie's pardon, three men were put to death, one after another, in the electric chair at Sing Sing. The nervous strain which always accompanies an execution extended through the prison and the warden's house, even to Blackie's sick-room. In the cold gray dawn, as the fatal hour approached, Blackie became more and more restless. His faithful friend and biographer, Mrs. Field, coming to his bedside, heard him praying; and immediately afterward wrote down, so that it should not be forgotten, this eloquent cry to God from the lips of the man who was himself so soon to die:

> "O God, if I could only be taken instead of those three young men in the full vigor of their strength! There is work for them to do on this earth, even behind the bars, while my course is run. The sand in my hourglass has only a few grains left, and they are rapidly slipping through. But — Thy will be done! And if they

are to go and I am to stay, even for a little while, may it be for some great and high purpose. O God, in spite of the past, make the life of each man within the walls count for something! May the passing out of these three brave souls today mean also the passing out of that old medieval law of capital punishment. Bless all my pals everywhere."

On the 20th of March, 1915, Blackie died of the tuberculosis contracted during his long confinement in the cold, stone dark-cell of Clinton prison. He died, one of the many thousands of martyrs of the brutal old prison system. How many men, one wonders, of equal capacity for right living and high thinking, have perished as criminals when they might have lived as upbuilders of humanity? No one can tell. The secrets of the past, in the dark-cells of Clinton, Sing Sing, Auburn, Wethersfield, and other old prisons will never be revealed; we can only guess. In this case it fortunately happened that such a man was imprisoned where his soul could catch the light, where he could share in the first fine enthusiasm of a new freedom, and find joy in the glow and fervor of a new life. He was able to use his great influence, (for Blackie was a veritable hero of the underworld — he bore a name to conjure with), to help build first at Auburn and later at Sing Sing the broad and strong foundations of a new penology; a prison system which should appeal to all that is best in the inmates, instead of degrading all to the level of the worst.

The very qualities which had made this man one of the most dangerous of criminals — his skill, ingenuity, boldness, bravery, intellectual power, and loyalty — ("the whitest of pals" is the way one friend has described him): all those things were assets of the highest value to society, the moment he turned to "go straight." The dangerous and desperate criminal is often only the hero gone wrong.

Back in Prison—Why?
(An Excerpt)

by
Donald Lowrie

"Back in Prison— Why?"

by
Donald Lowrie

FINDS ANOTHER
EXCUSE FOR DRINK

HEADS FOR GREAT SEAL
TO BE ATTACHED

Back in Prison—Why?

Life at Sing Sing was so kaleidoscopic during the months of 1915, with what seemed like important happenings crowded into the background almost daily by happening of still greater import, that my mind now refuses to give chronological sequence.

I shall, therefore, set down such events as stand out in my recollection, and in which I played my part. These may not be, probably are not, the most important things to record, so far as a history of Sing Sing during that period is concerned, but I have recently learned such a history is now being written by Tom Osborne himself.[1]

Sing Sing entombed a number of "prominent" prisoners who had lived in "Bankers' Row" and enjoyed many private privileges. It had been the custom of the politicians who controlled the prison to make life as easy as possible for thieves in the five, six, or seven-figure class — offenders who had wrecked financial institutions or gotten away with thousands of dollars of other people's money through high finance.

[1] Sadly, Osborne passed away before completing that book.

This applied especially to those who had retained their spoils and were able to buy prison "favor."

When Osborne took charge, for example, there was a high-powered automobile in the garage, the property of a convict who had bought it for the warden's use, with the understanding that he, the convict, was to be the chauffeur. This man had been permitted to drive to New York and other places almost at will, until disaster came through publicity.

Other "bon tons," however, were still enjoying special privileges and favors, and, in a way, ruled the prison.

Osborne determined to change all this, not by arbitrary action — though that was justified — but through the influence of the prisoners' organization, in which every man had a voice. As a result, it very soon became apparent that out-and-out burglars had more principle and a better conception of true social values than had in-and-out bankers and other captured wolves of finance. The "prominence" of the "silk stocking" class soon faded, so far as the prison was concerned, and hitherto obscure prisoners began to rise to the top by sheer force of ability and inherent character.

And be it said in passing that in the workings of prison self-government the stool pigeons and four-flushers[2] had no chance to pursue their evil practices. They became non-entities, creatures openly despised by all.

Among men thus forced to the top, where they could be most useful to themselves and their fellow, were "Canada Blackie," and "Billy" Duffy. Of course there were others, including, "Charlie" Newman, George Hodson, "Dick" Richards, and "O.K. Bill."

Richards had as keen a mind as any man I have ever known, with a memory and a capacity for analysis that would have carried him far in the realms of legitimate enterprise outside. Blackie I had first met at Auburn prison, where I found him in solitary confinement, in the "incorrigible" ward.

[2] Deceivers; bluffers; cheaters.

He had been in prison twelve years and in "solitary" five years. He was of the slender, wiry type, with black hair, turned gray, and determined eyes and chin. He reminded me very much of my friend, Jack Black, in San Francisco — he from whom I had "escaped" that night at the Older ranch when my friends had induced him to act as "jailer" over me in an effort to keep me from further drinking.[3]

Blackie looked and talked like Jack, and had much of the same wonderful philosophy and strength of character. At first, peering out at me from his solitary cell, Blackie had taken me for a "prison reformer" — he told me so — but when I told him I had "done time" and other things about myself, he had "loosened up" and we became friends.

Blackie had subsequently been released from the isolation ward at Auburn through the intercession of Osborne, and had within a very short time been elected by the prisoners as an officer of the Mutual Welfare League. Blackie had contracted tuberculosis while in solitary confinement at Clinton prison, some years before, and the disease had reached that stage where there seemed no hope of its arrest or his recovery if he remained in prison.

To attempt getting a pardon for him seemed hopeless. He had been sentenced to life imprisonment, and later to ten years additional. The life sentence had been imposed following his conviction of having participated in a country bank robbery at night, in the perpetration of which one of his companions had shot and killed a watchman.

Two of the gang had been electrocuted, and had, of course, long ceased to suffer. Blackie had later made a desperate attempt to escape from Clinton prison, and had been taken to court for that offense and given ten extra years — a farcical proceeding. He had since come down through the dreary years with each month adding to his pain and hopelessness.

[3] Jack Black (1871–1932) was a professional burglar best known for his 1926 autobiography *You Can't Win*. Lowrie details the episode mentioned in Chapter 26 of *Back in Prison—Why?*

It was some time during January of 1915 that Osborne secured Blackie's transfer from Auburn to Sing Sing in the hope that the change of climate might be beneficial, and because Blackie, with a former reputation as the "most dangerous and desperate convict in New York State," had developed such a powerful influence for good among the Auburn prisoners that it was hoped his presence at Sing Sing might have similar result, notwithstanding his much impaired physique.

Billy Duffy, Blackie's best friend and helper had also been transferred to Sing Sing, to act as nurse — for Blackie was then remaining on his feet day after day only by sheer force of will. I renewed my friendship with Blackie at Sing Sing, where I also came to regard Billy Duffy as one of the strongest factors within the walls for bringing the self-government system to its highest point of efficiency.

Nor was I wrong. It was Duffy, former sergeant-at-arms of the league at Auburn, who trained George Hodson for a similar job at Sing Sing, and it was Hodson who, sometime later, averted a panic and a possible delivery of the prison.

This occurred one night while the prisoners were assembled in the chapel on the second floor of the long building used as a mess hall, when a fire broke out in the cellar, or storerooms, underneath. The fire had gained much headway before it was discovered, and the first intimation to those in the chapel of anything wrong was when the lights suddenly went out, just after a white-faced prisoner had hurried from the rear and up to the platform, where he whispered something to Hodson, who was in charge of the meeting.

Coincident with the extinguishment of lights came the smell of smoke, the flicker of flames on the windows and excited voices in the prison yard below. Everyone instantly realized there was a fire, and for an awful instant a panic seemed inevitable. Then came a voice — the voice of Convict George Hodson — talking in the dark.

"It's a test!" he cried. "A test of whether we're really men or not! Don't get excited. If we mess things up the news-papers will jump all over us — call us cowards and all that. Begin at the back and march out and every man go direct to his cell — no fooling, now! Remember, we're all men, every one of us."

Before he finished speaking the men were on their feet, slowly working their way down the double aisles toward the one egress at the rear, where a wooden stairway led down to the dining room below. There was no crowding, no excite-ment. Swarms of men shuffled past in the dark, talking in low voices, wondering how "bad" the fire was. The smoke was getting dense. Long before the chapel was emptied the men were coughing.

In the dining room below the crowd was obliged to wait while comrades were counted, one by one, through a narrow doorway at the far end, leading to the cell block.

Meanwhile, flames had burst from the cellar windows underneath, and the smoke had increased until breathing was very difficult. Finally the last man was counted through that narrow door. A few minutes later the lock-up count was checked by the principal keeper, and it was found that every prisoner was accounted for. Not one had taken advantage of the darkness and confusion to attempt escape or to make disturbance. All save those engaged in fighting the fire were in their cells. Yet, only the year before Osborne's advent the prisoners at Sing Sing had mutinied and set fire to the shops in protest against intolerable conditions.

During the time I remained at Sing Sing I never saw any-thing more conclusive of the value of self-government than what occurred that night. George Hodson, a convict, had, by use of a few well chosen, intensely spoken words, quelled that awful mob-fear common in all human emergencies, where many persons are crowded together in face of danger, and the convicts, appealed to on the ground of "acting like men and justifying trust," had responded, without a single exception.

ch. ends p. 96

It took more than two hours to conquer that fire, the convict firemen crawling in through the smoke with hose and sticking to it like veterans. When one group came out, wet, black, and choking, another group took up the battle. Without the prisoners' work that night, the kitchen, mess hall, and chapel would have been destroyed.

Yet there were many outside scoffers at the self-government system, and today, notwithstanding conclusive proofs, that men given responsibilities are made stronger and better thereby, these scoffers remain, and gain more attention than those who have given the matter years of close study. I sometimes think it is the willingness on the part of the public to believe the worst of the wrongdoer that drives me back to evil ways after they have paid prison penalties. I know, in my own case, down through the years, that the advocacy of "more punishment" for prisoners, indulged in by many newspaper editors, had been a source of discouragement to me, making me feel that the sacrifice of my own life and privacy — where I would not have become prominent, and might therefore never have been pulled down — has been a big price to pay for others.

I found the men at Sing Sing eager to do right, anxious to better themselves, and surprisingly imbued with that principle of group preservation upon which our civilization stands.

✳

I have mentioned "Canada Blackie" and his transfer from Auburn prison to Sing Sing on account of his health, and because Osborne felt the need of his influence to promote the best interests of the Sing Sing prisoners.

Soon after Blackie's arrival, in January, his tubercular condition became much worse, compelling him to remain in bed. There was some talk of transferring him to Clinton prison, in the Adirondack region, but Blackie balked at the plan, pleading to remain near his "friend, Tom," meaning Osborne.

Some time previous, while Blackie was still at Auburn, I think it was, on learning of the man's grave illness, Governor Whitman had voluntarily declared that he would not let Blackie die in prison; that, in view of his wonderful comeback for good and his excellent influence at Auburn following his release from "solitary," he, the governor, would pardon him, provided he was assured there was no hope of the prisoner's recovery.

When Blackie declined to be transferred to Clinton prison, Tom arranged for his comfort in a special room on the top floor of the warden's residence. The sick man was carried up and installed there, with Billy Duffy as his nurse. After that, at all hours of the day and night, Blackie's wracking cough kept us reminded of his approaching death, making life tragic and more burdensome than ever.

Not that any of us thought of it in that way, for we all liked Blackie tremendously, and were willing to do anything in the world for him. It is only now, as I look back in the effort to understand what happened to myself and to explain it, that I see how Blackie's wretched ending affected me, and gave me additional excuse for seeing solace and night oblivion in whiskey.

Mrs. Annie P. L. Field, of Brooklyn, became deeply interested in Blackie's case, and came to Sing Sing every other day to read and cheer the stricken man. Mrs. Field subsequently became the author of *The Story of Canada Blackie*, a book which had wide circulation in the East. Day by day it became more and more certain that Blackie was doomed, until along in the middle of March I was one morning dispatched to Albany, bearing certificates from two doctors to the effect that Blackie had but a few days of life left.

A specialist, called from New York by Osborne a few days before, had taken one hasty look at the patient's throat and

ch. ends p. 96

refrained from further examination, declaring afterward that there was absolutely no hope.

To see our friend sink lower and lower, always smiling or trying to smile, when conscious, had been a hard ordeal.

I arrived at Albany, the capital, determined that if it were in my power to secure the pardon I would leave no stone unturned.

It was just before noon when I was received by the governor. Briefly but forcefully as possible I stated my mission and handed him the doctors' certificates. I remained standing before Whitman's desk, not having been invited to take a seat. As he looked over the documents I studied him. His face was that of a fighter, with heavy jaws and cold eyes — gray or blue eyes, I'm not sure which. I remembered his bulldog determination in the Rosenthal murder prosecution, and how his name had figured in the daily newspaper reports during the trial of "the four gunmen," already electrocuted, and his vigorous, bitter prosecution of Charles Becker, the New York police lieutenant who at that very moment was awaiting the "chair" in the death house within Sing Sing walls.

It had been that case — the prosecution of those charged with responsibility for Rosenthal's murder — that had "made" Whitman and won for him the governorship of New York State.

I could not help feeling as I stood there before him, that he had been elevated to high office on a sort of fluke, without ever having evinced any real executive or administrative ability. Suddenly he looked up at me. I do not think he knew who I was, i.e. my claim to authorship and my lecturing on prison facts. I felt quite sure he took me to be merely a clerk at the prison.

"What do you think of this case?" he asked, in what seemed to be a half petulant tone. "I've already passed my word to issue a pardon when his case became hopeless — which is not evidently is. But what will be the result? His offense was a particularly grave one."

"It will have a very beneficial result, so far as the prisoners are concerned," I declared, as impressively as I could. "He had the reputation of being the most dangerous convict in the state. He turned straight, became as good as he had been bad, and swayed hundreds of others to do likewise. He can't live to benefit from a pardon, but every prisoners in the state of New York, and many in other states, will realize there is such a thing as recognition of and reward for right, and all they've ever known hitherto has been the certainty of punishment for wrong. His pardon will mean a great deal toward prison discipline."

The governor touched a button and asked me to be seated. Presently Potter, the pardon clerk, an ascetic looking man whom I had seen before, and who had a reputation among the prisoners as "a hard nut," appeared. "Fill out a pardon for this man," ordered Whitman, indicating the name on the doctors' certificate. "Bring it to me at once."

Potter withdrew, and Whitman asked me how things were going on at Sing Sing. I told him they couldn't better under the circumstances.

"What do you mean by 'circumstances'?" he demanded.

The rat-hole cells, the poorly ventilated shops, the over-crowding, the damp walls," I replied. "New York needs an open-air prison, the kind where men will be regenerated and——"

I was interrupted by the reappearance of Potter, who told the governor in what seemed a satisfied tone that Blackie had two commitments, and innocently (?) inquired which offense the pardon was to cover.

Whitman was surprised. He turned to me half accusatively, or so it seemed. Apparently he was piqued that he had not been acquainted with all the facts of the case.

Briefly I told him the circumstances — the extra sentence

of ten years imposed at Plattsburg for Blackie's attempted escape from Clinton prison.

"I didn't agree to issue two pardons," declared Whitman. "I knew nothing of this other commitment."

"But you agreed to pardon the man, and that's the point," I replied. "Every prisoner in Sing Sin and Auburn knows of that promise. You'll — you'll have to keep your word, Governor."

He glared at me.

"You prison officials are getting altogether too sentimental," he grumbled. "I don't know where it will all end. But you're right. I gave my promise."

He turned to Potter.

"Make out two pardons, one for each case," he ordered.

Much to my secret elation, Potter started to offer some technical objection. In the brief time I had observed Whitman I knew, or felt, that opposition was the very thing that would make him determined, nor was I wrong.

"Get the two pardons ready!" he snapped.

Potter retired again, and Whitman began reading from a typewritten document on his desk. At last Potter returned, bearing two long sheets of parchment, which he smoothed out before the executive. Whitman glanced over them hastily and then dashed off his name, twice. I wanted to reach for the documents and must have made an involuntary movement to do so.

"They've got to have the great seal affixed first," said Potter. "It will take only a minute."

I arose and thanked the governor.

"Perhaps you'd like to telephone to the prison," he suggested, considerately. "I suppose they'll like to know, especially the beneficiary. You'll find a booth in the next room."

I thanked him again and withdrew. In the telephone booth I got Malloy, the chief clerk at the prison on the line. Osborne, I learned, had gone to New York, and Johnson, the deputy warden, was somewhere inside the prison.

"Well, tell Johnson, I've got Blackie's pardon, all right,"
I said exultantly. "But in my judgment it should be Osborne
who should take the good news to him. Tell Johnson I suggest
that."

An hour later I was speeding down the Hudson on a fast
train. By mid-afternoon I was back the prison, where I found
Mrs. Field in great excitement. She insisted that we ought
to advise Blackie at once of the pardon, and not wait for
Osborne's return. "It will brace him up!" she exclaimed.

I told her I had conceived what I considered a fine plan,
and felt sure Osborne would agree to it. "Let's be patient,"
I urged. "Let's have Billy Duffy, Blackie's pal, give him the
pardon, with Tom and you and myself and other friends all
present. I don't think such a thing as one convict handing a
pardon to another has ever happened in the prison history
of the world, and Blackie, I know, will appreciate it." I finally
made her see that my plan was good.

That night, when Osborne had returned, we all went up to
Blackie's bedside together, and Duffy, with trembling voice,
read the text of the pardons, and then reverently placed
the documents under the dying man's pillow. Blackie was
too weak to talk. Only his eyes showed his gratitude. It was
indeed a case of "the pardon that came too late."

✳

It was about 4 o'clock on the morning of March 20, 1915,
when Blackie died, less than a week after receiving his pardon.[4] I had been up, along with Harry and Jack, until about
2 o'clock and when Duffy woke me and told me the end had
come, I got up again.

We went down into the kitchen and made some black
coffee and talked about what we should do. Osborne and
Johnson were both absent from the prison, and I was virtually

[4] Blackie's entry in the Sing Sing registry lists the time of death as 7:10 a.m.

in charge. It was the first time in my life that I had faced the responsibility of making arrangements concerning a dead body. None of the boys seems to have had any experiences, either.

I knew Johnson was due back at the prison that morning early, so decided to go to New York and see Osborne, who was at the Belmont Hotel, having spoken in New York the night before, and scheduled to leave for Philadelphia at 8 o'clock, with his return to the prison fixed for that evening.

I advised Duffy not to disturb the body until the prison physician had seen it. In my room for a moment I swallowed a big drink of whiskey. Then I was driven to the Ossining station, where I caught the "flower" train for New York. The "flower" train went through each morning shortly before 5 o'clock, picking up freshly cut flowers from the numerous hothouse plants and nurseries all along the route, for delivery in the city. It carried one or two passenger coaches.

I arrived in New York shortly after 6 — too early to disturb Tom. I decided to wait until 7:30 or 8 before calling him up. My understanding was that he would take the 10 o'clock Pennsylvania train to Philadelphia.

At first I had breakfast in mind I was tired and unstrung. But instead of turning into the station restaurant I went down to the bar and had a drink of whiskey. After a few minutes I took another. Then I began to think, or thought I did. Why disturb Tom at all? It would only distress him to learn of Blackie's death. What could he do in the matter that I couldn't do, anyway? There was really no sense in my having come to New York. I would take the next train back.

I had two or three more drinks and then returned to Sing Sing, arriving at the prison before 9 o'clock. Johnson had not returned. Blackie's body was still lying in the bed where he had died.

I learned that someone had called up Mrs. Field, and that she was one her way to the prison from Brooklyn. Mrs. Field was very emotional. I knew there would be a scene.

I felt it was necessary to have the remains moved before she got there.

I called up the undertaker at Ossining. He response was prompt. In less than half an hour he called and removed the body to his mortuary in the village. All that morning was turmoil. Mrs. Field arrived and became hysterical. She upbraided me for not having waited until she got there before having the body taken away. I told her Blackie had looked terrible — which he had — and that I felt it better that the undertaker should make the remains presentable before she or anyone else saw them. She went down to the village. I slipped up to my room for more whiskey.

It was not until lunch time that I awoke to the fact of a lecture engagement I had for 3 o'clock that afternoon in New York. The Women's Equal Suffrage League was at that time holding daily afternoon meeting at it quarters in Fifth Avenue and advertising a different speaker each day.

Mrs. Chadbourne, one of the live wires of the organization, had been at Sing Sing some days before and had secured my promise to speak on the afternoon of March 20. Osborne, by the way, was opposed to equal suffrage at that time, but came over later. His attitude on that question was being used against him by his enemies.

When my promise to speak that afternoon occurred to me my first impulse was to cancel the engagement by telephone. I had been missing sleep for several nights, and the events of the day had been nerve-sapping. But after eating lunch I felt better and decided to go. It was understood that I was to take dinner at the Chadbourne residence after the lecture, and attend a theater party that night.

I packed my evening clothes in a suitcase and caught a train for New York, which delivered me at the Grand Central terminal with just barely time enough to get to the lecture hall.

My address proved wretched. My brain refused to work. Besides, it was a new subject with me. I got through somehow,

ch. ends p. 96

and was followed by a speaker from Boston who had his facts splendidly arrayed and made up for my deficiency. Then followed the usual hour of talk with groups that came up to the platform — one of the severest ordeals that public lecturers have to go through — and the ride to Mrs. Chadbourne's home accompanied by the Boston lecturer and our hostess.

I have forgotten the Boston gentleman's name, but vividly recall that he patronizingly gave me oodles of advice on "how to talk before the public" as the vehicle proceeded slowly up Fifth Avenue. That embarrassed me, especially with Mrs. Chadbourne present. Several time she tactfully tried to change the subject, evidently sensing my displeasure, but the man from Boston kept right on.

Before we reached our destination I wanted to jump out of the machine and run. The thought of sitting through a formal dinner and listening to the same monotone for an hour or so appalled me.

When we arrived at the house Mrs. Chadbourne informed us that dinner would be at 7, and I was escorted by a servant to a room where there was a bath. It was then about 6. Soon as I was alone I ran my fingers through my hair in nervous frenzy. I was at the breaking point. I had not really relaxed my mind or body for over a week.

The thought of the coming dinner, when I would be supposed to be "brilliant," or at least "interesting," weighed heavily upon me. Nor did the proposed theater party afterward, to see "The Lion and the Mouse," offer any lure.

I felt that I couldn't stand any more — that I must get off by myself. Above all, my whole body was shrieking for alcohol, for something that would quiet my nerves quickly.

I stood in the center of the room for a long time, thinking. My suitcase was there. I was supposed to be dressing for dinner. I spied a desk and writing material. I sat down and penned a hasty note to Mrs. Chadbourne, pleading sudden indisposition and asked to be excused. Then I got my suitcase, went out into the hall, left the note conspicuously on a stand — I don't know whether it was ever found or not, nor just what happened when I failed to show up for dinner — and descended the stairs.

A moment later I was on the street, going fast as I could toward Broadway — and a saloon. It was only after I had taken several stiff drinks or whiskey that I felt normal. And awful temptation came over me to go to a hotel and drink from a bottle, but I smothered it down. I got back to Sing Sing before 9 o'clock. Tom had returned. He told me he was well pleased with the way I had handled the situation in his absence. I went to bed quite early.

Three or four days later Jack, the chauffeur, and I drove to the crematory for Blackie's ashes. To my utter confusion, mixed with a feeling or horror, I was handed a tin can, sealed, and with a slip of paper pasted across the top bearing Blackie's name. I took it in my hand gingerly after signing a receipt and walked out to the car.

"What the matter, isn't he ready?" asked Jack as I approached. "What's that you've got in your hand?"

"It's Blackie," I said resentfully, proffering the can to him.

"No, no — I don't want it. Take it away!" he half shouted, crouching against the farther side of the car. "Gee, but that's fierce. Where're we going to put it?"

His shrinking attitude amused me. I suddenly saw the funny side of the situation.

"We could give him the entire back seat," I laughed, "but let's be sociable. Let's let him sit between us."

I climbed in and placed the can on the seat close to Jack. As I did something rattled inside, and Jack nearly leaped from the vehicle.

"My God! What was that?" he gasped.

The noise had startled me, too. It seemed uncanny. I also made an involuntary movement to get out — and walk home. Then I happened to remember poor Blackie's gold fillings. That was it, of course. There was gold in the ashes. The dross had burned away — the gold was left. I tried to say something religious to that effect — something about the gold in Blackie's character surviving even death, but it went over Jack's head, I think.

"Well," he said resignedly, "this is a new one on me, but it's all in a lifetime. I'll be glad when we get him home."

A few days later elaborate funeral services for Blackie were held in Sing Sing prison, the can of ashes being covered with velvet and placed in a mahogany box, beautifully inlaid with abalone. These services were later repeated at Auburn prison, and then the little casket, bearing an appropriate inscription, was buried in a private plot at Auburn.

I did not attend either of these services. Much as I had liked Blackie, and much as I revered his strength of character and fortitude under suffering, the lure of whiskey proved too much.

The Sunday Blackie's funeral was held at Sing Sing I was drunk. And although as an honorary member of the Mutual Welfare League I was invited to accompany the remains to Auburn and attend the services there, I declined.

For a period of several days I had been going about with my head awhirl, there were moments when I really feared I might be going crazy. The only thing to give me relief from my tense condition was whiskey, and I drank lots of it.

In the News

Leader Among Criminals
the Wreck of a Genius

Canada Blackie, Now Dead, So Strong of Mind That Years of Solitary Confinement Failed to Crush Him—Cracksman Might Have Been Financier.

By LEWIS WOOD.

The ashes of "Canada Blackie," who died in the warden's house at Sing Sing Saturday, will reach the prison today. But they will not stay long in this one of the prisons the man spent so much of his life in. It will only be a short time before they are taken to Auburn and buried in a plot provided by Thomas Mott Osborne.

I met Blackie—John Murphy was his name—when I did a voluntary bit in Sing Sing in January. My impressions of the man were lasting then. As I grew to know him better I was more and more impressed with the man's vivid personality. He had been in prison—this time—twelve years, and he had seventeen years ahead of him. But two things intervened—death and a merciful pardon. Tuberculosis had the man in its grip for months, and it laid him on his back a few weeks ago. It was then Governor Whitman issued him a pardon, of which he was deadly proud.

The first time I ever saw this man was in the prison yard in Sing Sing. He was in the hospital even then, but he used to come out in the yard an hour or two each day. He wanted to keep on his feet as long as he could.

Once a Giant.

It was in the middle of January. Half a week later he went to bed for keeps. Ever since then he had been dying by inches, fighting death as if it were something you could grasp in your hands.

He walked up that day a great, gaunt, raw-boned man. He must have stood well over 6 feet before consumption sunk his head and bowed his shoulders. He must have weighed 200 pounds before prison and disease broke down his powerful physique.

Steady eyes, as keen and sharp as knives, looked out from beneath brows masked with bushy iron-gray hair. A strong, firm-lipped mouth, a straight nose and high cheekbones their clear

when he was in solitary. He had been there five years then—five years in a little cell. Guards would take two of them out to put him in line with them while he walked to the cell they kept quite close to him . . .

. . . decision with his characteristic . . . It was a . . .

Blackie . . . one of . . . this . . . He wanted to drill . . . safe door . . . he drilled the cracks with . . . filed them with a . . . away for the gold . . . hands. He took . . . think from the . . .

. . . shook his head . . . He got away and tried . . . The thumping . . . had been marked. And then he fled and tried it once more . . . turned it . . . the clicked! It was the last turn . . . stood erect and she clicked . . . it was the door, snapped his fingers like a railway torpedo. Achievement!

Before the time for the attempt to escape was ripe, "Tom Brown" Osborne went to see Blackie and won his confidence. At last, one day he went into Canada's cell and threw himself on the bed.

"Did you mean what you said the other day that you were going to let me out of here? Did you really mean it?" asked Blackie.

"Why, certainly," replied Mr. Osborne.

Blackie pressed Osborne. He could hardly believe he was going out of solitary. Finally the convict went over to a little stand and took up a box of talcum powder. He lifted off the lid and shook out the powder on the floor. In the middle of it was a little package wrapped in tissue paper. He handed this to Mr. Osborne, who unwrapped it. It was the key and the file!

Another one of his experiences at this time—he called it his birthday, "the time I was born on earth again,"

Leader Among Criminals the Wreck of a Genius

Canada Blackie, Now Dead, So Strong of Mind That Years of Solitary Confinement Failed to Crush Him — Cracksman Might Have Been Financier

The ashes of "Canada Blackie," who died in the warden's house at Sing Sing Saturday, will reach the prison today. But they will not stay long in this one of the prisons the man spent so much of his life in. It will only be a short time before they are taken to Auburn and buried in a plot provided by Thomas Mott Osborne.

I met Blackie — John Murphy was his name — when I did a voluntary bit in Sing Sing in January.[1] My impressions of the man were lasting then. As I grew to know him better I was more and more impressed with the man's vivid personality. He had been in prison — this time — twelve years, and he had seventeen years ahead of him. But two things intervened — death and a merciful pardon, of which he was rightly proud.

---

[1] Journalist Lewis Wood voluntarily spent three days as an inmate in Sing Sing and wrote a story about his experience: Sing Sing Prison Under Osborne's Reform Conditions: An Intimate Study of Cell Life. (1915, January 18). *New-York Tribune*, 74(24900), pp. A1; A5.

The first time I ever say this man was in the prison yard in Sing Sing. He was in the hospital even then, but he used to come out in the yard and hour or two each day. He wanted to keep on his feet as long as he could.

It was in the middle of January. Half a week later he went to bed for keeps. Ever since then he had been dying by inches, fighting death as if it were something you could grasp in your hands.

He walked up that day a great, gaunt, raw-boned man. He must have stood well over 6 feet before consumption sank his head and bowed his shoulders. He must have weighed 200 pounds before prison and disease broke down his powerful physique.

Steady eyes, as keen and sharp as knives, looked out from beneath brows masked with bushy iron-gray hair. A strong, firm-lipped mouth, a straight nose and high cheekbones, their elevation accentuated by cheeks that had begun to sink, made up this man's face. (There's a big traffic policeman in Fourth Avenue that's just Blackie's type.) When he shook hands the curve between his thumb and forefinger went hard up to the curve between mine, and his long fingers closed strongly about my hand.

The man's whole note was dominant. There was something electric about this quality he had. He was purposeful and a leader. Once he said when he was a small boy his mother wanted him to be a priest. Well, he would have been a strong one. I used to think sometimes Blackie would have made a great bank president if he had not been a bank burglar.

It was his strength that enabled him to lie a night and a day in the deep woods with a bullet hole through his jaw.[2] It was this strength that carried him through years of prison life that would have wrecked the brain of a weaker man.

He lived twenty months in a dark cell at Dannemora. They stowed him away in solitary confinement at Auburn for five mortal years. He lived through the hell of Joliet. But he

[2] This article is the only source that we could find of this bit of information.

never gave in. He fought back. He would have been fighting back to the day of his death against the brutal treatment and injustice of the old prison system if a man had not happened along and begun to treat him as if he were a human being.

He talked a long time that night to Mr. Johnson, the deputy warden, and Donald Lowrie and me, and his nurse, a sturdy, broad-shouldered chap with a small waist and narrow, close hips and a quick lifting walk, just like a middleweight prizefighter.

That was the first time Canada ever told the story of how he made the key when he was in solitary. He had been there five years then — five years in a little cell. Once a week keepers took him out, guarding him with clubs while he walked to the baths. They kept quite close to him. He was "a bad man," you see. No one else ever came in the solitary, no one except the guards. And so, after a while, Canada decided to get away. He made his decision with his characteristic fatalism. It was a long chance — there were many doors, there were guards with guns and there was a wall — but anything was better than the doom of prison, better than solitary, better than the coolers, where he threw buttons into the air and groped for them in the dark to keep from going mad.

Blackie set to work to make his key with the same nerve, patience, and deliberation he used to drill a safe door before he filled the cracks with "soup," muffled the door with a carpet and blew it away for the gold and greenbacks inside. He took a piece of steel. I never knew where it came from, but I think from his shoe.

He told how he stretched his hand between the bars of the door and tried the key blank in the lock time and again. Each time he looked to see if the lampblack on it had been marked. And then he filed and filed it. And at last one day it worked.

"I turned it, and she clicked! It was the half turn! I edged over, and she clicked again! It was the double turn!" As he said "turn" he snapped his fingers like a railway torpedo. Achievement!

Before the time for the attempt to escape was ripe "Tom

Brown" Osborne went to see Blackie and won his confidence. At last, one day he went into Canada's cell and threw himself on the bed.

"Did you mean what you said the other day — that you were going to let me out of here? Did you really mean it?" asked Blackie.

"Why, certainly," replied Mr. Osborne.

Blackie pressed Osborne. He could hardly believe he was going out of solitary. Finally the convict went over to a little stand and took up a box of talcum powder. He lifted the lid and shook out the powder on the floor. In the middle of it was a little package wrapped in tissue paper. He handed this to Mr. Osborne, who unwrapped it. It was the key and the file!

Another one of his experiences at this time — he called it his birthday, "the time I was born on earth again" — was described in a letter to a friend, a letter so vivid and interesting that Thomas W. Churchill, president of the Board of Education, wishes to have it published. It was his first talk with a woman. It had been a long day since Blackie had talked to a woman. Mrs. Anne P. L. Field, of Brooklyn, an author, interested in prison work, was visiting Auburn and had sung to the prisoners. She saw Blackie stalking about the yard and was interested in this tragic figure.

"I want to talk to that man," she said to Mrs. Charles Osborne, Thomas Mott Osborne's daughter-in-law.

"Well, you'll have a hard time; he's said to be a woman hater," laughed Mrs. Osborne.

But in the end Mrs. Field did talk to Canada. And she won his friendship and confidence. Every week since he was taken ill she visited the prison and read to the man and talked to him. Her influence with him has brought out his best side, so Warden Osborne says, the side which was always there, but which was repressed and shut up in his bitter fight.

I saw much of the "best side" of this man. He was loyal and brave and generous. The first time I saw him he had a pair of low shoes. It was January. And he was coughing.

I did not find out until two days after that Blackie had seen a man in the yard with a broken pair of shoes, and given away his own.

"Well, I didn't need the high ones. I'm in bed most of the time, anyway," was what he told his pal in explanation.

There was a photograph of a young woman on the table beside Blackie's bedside. Nobody knew who it was. Another photograph of her, a snapshot taken in California, showed her in the front seat of an automobile. It would have been easy to trace the number. But who wanted to ferret out the man's secret?

Lewis Wood
New-York Tribune
March 24, 1915

opposition to the measure.

President Churchill said he was certain the Board of Education intended to go on record against the bill unless it was amended to give the board the power it now possesses to increase but not to decrease salaries. He said the Board of Education would fight to maintain the present system of payment for teachers.

the idea of making a personal inspection of all the institutions where the city's poor are cared for," said Mr. Kingsbury, "and if I should visit one place every day, including Sundays and holidays, at the end of a year I would not be quite through with my inspection. This will give you some idea of the magnitude of the Department of Charities.

SING SING PRISONERS WEEP AT CANADA BLACKIE'S BIER

Warden Osborne Almost in Tears as He Pronounces Eulogy of Convict, Who Made Good in Aiding Mutual Welfare League.

There never was a funeral in prison before like that of Canada Blackie's at Sing Sing, yesterday. The whole prison turned out to do honor to a man whose strength of character, once turned to a right end, played a leading part in molding the Mutual Welfare League at Sing Sing and at Auburn into a medium working for good in prisoners' lives.

Some 1,600 men stood, bareheaded, in the sunshine of the yard while John Murphy's ashes were carried to the chapel. The prison band, playing a dead march, led the procession. Members of the league carried a bier on which rested the ashes inclosed in an inlaid wood box made by a convict in Auburn. A great wreath lay on the black cloth that hid the box. In the centre of the wreath was the league badge of which Blackie was so proud.

Warden Osborne walked behind with some of the man's intimate friends. Some were prisoners. Others were Mrs. Anne T. L. Field, of Brooklyn, who was such an influence on Murphy's later life; Miss Madeline Z. Doty, "Bob" Cameron, who "came back" after twelve years in Auburn prison, and "Ed" Morrell, who is successful after years in San Quentin. Hundreds of little green and white "M. W. L." buttons and palm leaf crosses were pinned on the collars of gray prison coats.

The chapel was crowded. The service was impressive, and the prisoners were deeply touched, especially when Warden Osborne spoke and a poem, "More Light," by Mrs. Field, was read.

"If any man had a right to have a grudge against society, a right to wish to 'pay back' the world, Blackie had it," said the warden. "But no one has that right. And no one ever came to see that point of view more clearly than he did. He was considered the 'most dangerous prisoner in New York State.' May 1 Warden Kattigan was afraid to allow him to be alone with me for a talk. June 2 Blackie gave me the key he had made to open his cell and the knife he said he had intended to use in an attempt to escape. 'I'm going straight,' he said, and he never faltered afterward. He bent all the powers of a forceful, remarkable mind toward helping the league.

"One of the most characteristic incidents of Blackie's life occurred when the chaplain went to see him. Blackie didn't want any misunderstanding. 'I hope you don't think that, after what I've been and what I've done, I intend at this last minute to try to sneak into heaven,' he said. But, my friends, no one can 'sneak' into heaven. And Blackie has gone in by the front door."

Warden Osborne was so strongly affected he could not continue. Many of his hearers wept.

A message from Donald Lowrie, who spent ten years in San Quentin and knew Blackie well, was read by the warden. The Rev. Edgar F. Sanderson, of the Church of the Pilgrims, Brooklyn, conducted the services. Miss Leila Morse, of Rochester, sang, and Warden Osborne played her accompaniments.

The ashes will be taken, the last of this week, to Auburn for burial in Mr. Osborne's plot. Easter Sunday there will be a memorial service in Auburn prison, where Blackie spent five years in solitary confinement.

Sing Sing Prisoners Weep
at Canada Blackie's Bier

Warden Osborne Almost in Tears as He Pronounces Eulogy of Convict, Who Made Good in Aiding Mutual Welfare League

There never was a funeral in prison before like that of Canada Blackie's, at Sing Sing, yesterday. The whole prison turned out to do honor to a man whose strength of character, once turned to a right end, played a leading part in molding the Mutual Welfare League at Sing Sing and at Auburn into a medium working for good in prisoners' lives.

Some 1,600 men stood, bareheaded, in the sunshine of the yard while John Murphy's ashes were carried to the chapel. The prison band, playing a dead march, led the procession. Members of the league carried a bier on which rested the ashes enclosed in an inlaid wood box made by a convict in Auburn. A great wreath lay on the black cloth that hid the box. In the center of the wreath was the league badge of which Blackie was so proud.

Warden Osborne walked behind with some of the man's intimate friends. Some were prisoners. Others were Mrs. Anne P.L. Field, of Brooklyn, who was such an influence on

Murphy's later life; Miss Madeline Z. Doty, "Bob" Cameron, who "came back" after twelve years in Auburn prison, and "Ed" Morrell, who is successful after years in San Quentin. Hundreds of little green and white "M. W. L." buttons and palm leaf crosses were pinned on the collars of gray prison coats.

The chapel was crowded. The service was impressive, and the prisoners were deeply touched, especially when Warden Osborne spoke and a poem, "More Light," by Mrs. Field, was read.

"If any man had a right to have a grudge against society, a right to wish to 'pay back' the world, Blackie had it," said the warden. "But no one has that right. And no one ever came to see that point of view more clearly than he did. He was considered the 'most dangerous prisoner in New York State.' May 1, Warden Rattigan was afraid to allow him to be alone with me for a talk. June 2, Blackie gave me the key he had made to open his cell and the knife he said he had intended to use in an attempt to escape. 'I'm going straight,' he said, and he never faltered afterward. He bent all the powers of a forceful, remarkable mind toward helping the league.

"One of the most characteristic incidents of Blackie's life occurred when the chaplain went to see him. Blackie didn't want any misunderstanding. 'I hope you don't think that, after what I've been and what I've done, I intend at this last minute to try to sneak into heaven,' he said. But, my friends, no one can 'sneak' into heaven. And Blackie has gone in by the front door."

Warden Osborne was so strongly affected he could not continue. Many of his hearers wept.

A message from Donald Lowrie, who spent ten years in San Quentin and knew Blackie well, was read by the warden. The Rev. Edgar F. Sanderson, of the Church of the Pilgrims, Brooklyn, conducted the services. Miss Leila Morse, of Rochester, sang, and Warden Osborne played her accompaniments.

The ashes will be taken the last of this week to Auburn for burial in Mr. Osborne's plot. Easter Sunday there will be a memorial service in Auburn prison, where Blackie spent five years in solitary confinement.

New-York Tribune
March 29, 1915

FEDERATION HEARS OF PRISON REFORM

Federation Hears
of Prison Reform

Because the Social Center Association, which was to entertain the Federation of Women's Clubs at its quarterly general meeting on Saturday afternoon, had secured as the chief speaker Mrs. Anne P. L. Field of Brooklyn, who has been giving of herself and her means for prison reform work in this state, the chapel of the First Reformed Church was filled with eager listeners for this address.

*

Probably no woman present will ever forget the address given by Mrs. Anne P. L. Field on "Prison Reform."

At the close of her address, Dr. Day asked the speaker if, then, she believed in treating criminals as though they were normal human beings. The answer was instant, that she did not, any more than she believed in treating persons physically diseased as though they were physically normal. She believed in segregation of wrong-doers, and in punishment, but in punishment that should be educational and remedial; constructive, not destructive. And no human being should be treated as it would be impossible to treat an animal these days, without the rightful interference of both humane societies and society at large.

In telling of how she became interested, then active and now devoted to this cause of the outcast, Mrs. Field told the whole story of the present prison reform movement as inaugurated and carried forward by Thomas Mott Osborne, who was a college classmate and friend of her husband.[1]

As president of a Woman's Civic Club of Brooklyn, the speaker became generally interested in prison reform, and succeeded in getting Mr. Osborne to address that club. The fifty women who listened to Mr. Osborne from three to seven p.m. would never forget that afternoon, and Mrs. Field, "stabbed broad awake," became in 1914 a member of the Mutual Welfare League of the Prisons of New York. Doubtless because of her poise as well as depth of interest, over a year ago, Mr. Osborne invited her to visit his home and family in Auburn for five days (during which time he would be free) that she might know for herself the life at Auburn prison. Her husband readily consented to the visit and arriving at the Osborne home on Saturday, she first visited Auburn prison on a Sunday morning. In reply to her inquiry of Mr. Osborne as to why he had asked her, he told her she seemed peculiarly fitted for the work, and if she would take with the men at all she would take instantly and would never go back from the work. Otherwise she would have to go back home and embroider.

Accompanied by Mr. Osborne, she entered the prison, when some fifteen hundred men were assembled for a Sunday service, conducted by a Russian priest. The only woman in the room, she was separated from this body of convicts only by a brass railing, and the men that day, for the first, under their own guard. Mrs. Field described the experience

[1] Brooklyn-born and -practicing attorney Charles Merritt Field (1860–1916) died suddenly of acute indigestion at the couple's summer home in South Norwalk, Connecticut, on September 26, 1916. He was a Harvard grad, class of 1884; survived by Anne; a son of 19, Rowland; and a daughter several years younger, Elanor. On October 2, 1917, Anne married Dr. Thomas Mortimer Lloyd of Brooklyn.

as "volcanic." Just as they took their places on the steps, a man upon the stage drew aside the curtains, and at sight of Mrs. Field, faltered, stepped back, and disappeared. A little later, an attendant came and quietly spoke to Mr. Osborne, who seemed much concerned, and asked Mrs. Field if she would mind being left for a few moments. She thought of the "embroidery," and bravely answered "not at all." Before Mr. Osborne's return, the service was concluded, and that great body, in squads of fifty or sixty men, began marching toward her, quite naturally all eyes upon her. Just at first it seemed like standing upon the edge of a precipice, but then, nothing untoward happening, the speaker learned forever the needlessness of fear of these men, who are after all, men.

Returning, Mr. Osborne showed traces of deep emotion, and told Mrs. Field that the man who had drawn the curtains, and saw her suddenly, was "Canada Blackie," the most desperate criminal in the state. Her resemblance to his mother was so close, that the man whom neither torture nor solitary confinement could conquer, had utterly collapsed.

This was Mrs. Field's introduction to "Canada Blackie," although he would not consent to meet her face to face until some time after, knowing what an ordeal such a meeting would be. Mrs. Field considered the talk which she finally had with this criminal, (come from a mother of refinement and a father of intelligence but brutality when intoxicated), a man who might have been a genius because of the keenness of his mentality, alone in the warden's room at Auburn prison, to be the most extraordinary talk of her life. Standing on the brink of the grave, for during solitary confinement under conditions which would match those of many a Russian exile, "Canada Blackie" had lost sight of one eye (due to lack of light) and contracted tuberculosis of the throat and joints, this talk went to the elemental basis of everything in life.

For lack of something real to do, such as would content the live mind of a keen-witted boy, daring and wrong-doing full of excitement started this man at the early age of seven on the downward path. He was an educated and a clever

ch. ends next p

criminal whose desperate career might have been changed, if just once, "someone had cared."

After a period of solitary confinement at Dannemora, wherein the man nearly lost his reason, he was finally returned to Auburn, and here Mr. Osborne, visiting the prison one day, stopped at his cell, put his hand through the bars and offered to shake hands.

There was good excuse for Blackie's response, "What are you? One of those damned reformers?" Then relenting he shook hands with Mr. Osborne who proved to be the first person in many years who had spoken a kind word to him. So complete was Mr. Osborne's winning of the man, that soon after he gave him something for the warden, which proved to be a key to his cell which he had made, no one will ever know how,[2] and an ugly knife, which he had intended to use in one more dash for freedom.

Later Mr. Osborne visited this man in his cell and they talked of prison reform, and the inside knowledge of this man proved of great value. Later he was made an assistant sergeant-at-arms of the League, and was elected a delegate and placed on the executive committee. He became a great power for good in Auburn prison.

When the wardenship of Sing Sing was offered Mr. Osborne, he consulted with this man, who, with the voice of a prophet, told him that he dare not do otherwise than accept; that in spite of all that he would surely have to endure from the hands of his enemies, he was bound to give his life for the lives of the men in the prisons, and Mr. Osborne accepted. Mrs. Field made other visits to Auburn prison, learning to know Canada Blackie and his pals — looking at and listening to the woman, one realized what an influence she must have exerted, for she did not exact perfection; she did "understand."

When this prisoner became too ill to be about, he was brought to Sing Sing, Mr. Osborne then being warden, where he lived for three months in a little room on the third floor of

---

[2] But we do. (pp. 25, 105)

Mr. Osborne's home, attended by two pals as nurses. Here Mrs. Field, in her effort to make up for the nineteen years of mothering which the man had missed, visited him daily and for the last three weeks spent almost the entire part of each day with him, helping to care for him in his awful illness. She said in all sincerity and simplicity that never in her life had she been treated with such courtesy and reverence as during her stay at Sing Sing.

Finally Canada Blackie, pardoned by Governor Whitman, a free man, died, and according to his wishes his body was cremated, that it might be a menace to no one else. Under the new regime, the first funeral service ever held at Sing Sing was held on Palm Sunday, when Blackie's ashes, placed in an exquisitely inlaid box, the work of one of the prison men, was taken to the chapel, and a short but intensely impressive service was held. On the following Sunday, Easter, a memorial service was held at Auburn where the man was best known and loved; a service, which stood for the resurrection of all that is good. As the fourteen hundred prisoners carried the ashes to Fort Hill Cemetery,[3] where they found their final resting place, and stood there singing, "Lead Kindly Light, Amid the Encircling Gloom," it seemed indeed prophetic of a new era in the treatment of the outcast.

The Kingston Daily Freeman
January 17, 1916

---

[3] Fort Hill Cemetery is located in Auburn, New York. Thomas Mott Osborne is also buried there; the plain headstone features his name, dates of birth and death, and the emblem of the Mutual Welfare League.

to support a peace
ge
edge of events which
and have occurred,"
te. "it is not peace
thered by your move-
eting, but your pur-
the people of the
false position before
into the hands of
warring nations as

that emissaries of
ace had "gone from
insidious and false
empted to financially
mber of represents.
he union workers of
?"

IS IN OCTOBER

Will Be Docked at
Before Tests.

Sept. 2.—Arrange-
ial trials next month
Nevada comprised at
Shipbuilding Yards,
ced to-day. The N
drydock at Brook-
l. The speed trials
Penobscot course on
ill include the usual
d endurance runs,
of 27,000 tons car-
ries ten 14-inch guns,
es and four painting
r 21-inch submerged
he is similar to
ament, although 100

ERS:
ARSHIPS

LOWET, detached North
OWNALL, detached Aretic

A. DAVIDSON, detached
OORE, detached Centr to
detached North Dakota to
Neptune to
detached North Dakota

HOLDEN, detached
a Nat Home Warfare
CURTT
Barracks, Phila
YNON, to Mar. Barracks.

TCHELL, A. O. B. PUB-
ODE, J. A. McNAE, De

CANADA BLACKIE
AND PRISON REFORM

Mr. Osborne's Methods and an
Enemy of Society.

THE STORY OF CANADA BLACKIE. By Anne
... With an Introduction to Thomas
Mott Osborne ... pp. 197. E. P. Dutton & Co.

Canada Blackie died recently at Sing
Sing, a star exhibit of the results of
Mr. Osborne's prison methods. As a
boy the prisoner ran away from home
and joined a circus, which he deserted
after causing an accident that crippled
one of the performers (a woman) for
life. He then became the head of a
band of yeggmen, and served a term
in Joliet prison in the old days of
... Hungarian by ... with
and other methods of discipline.
He emerged from the penitentiary a
confirmed enemy of society, and went
in a safe-robbery in which a ...
was killed and wounded with ...
which he began at Dannemora prison,
for seven years. All round an ex-
ceptionable ... and his
endured six very ...
were satisfied ...
partly ... the
single ...

In his dark cell the man devised
... still more mysterious ... a
piece of magnin, which he ...
into a revolver, making the charge of
the hands of matches and the sides of
matchboxes. With this weapon he shot
a guard through the shoulder, the result being an additional sentence of
ten years. Altogether he spent twenty
months in the dark cell. Finally he was
transferred to Auburn, blind in one eye
and a victim of tuberculosis. Here he
met Donald Lowrie, the author of "My
Life in Prison" and "My Life Out of
Prison," and came under Mr. Osborne's
influence.

This is the story told in this book.
It is mostly made up, however, of
Blackie's letters to the Warden, to
Donald Lowrie and others. Of the re-

as his predecessor
out of the euphoria
contrast throughout
coarseness of these
fastidiousness of
iousness of body
there is her only so
not like the secon
upon him, and wh
over the fact that d
cied and cannot the
unwelcome intruder
which hit by her

"Shadows of Fla
of matrimonial ad
are now the ...
is implies of distill
revolt ... and com
... Macbeth
or Lord McGill
ister croaking out
... a million
over a million
ambly selected
interesting book

NICKY

NICKY-NAN, REE
Arthur Quiller-Co
... & Co.

Qr has broken t
a book that is a de
is a story of the
erange, and its ti
month of August,
are, therefore, as
fishermen, the vic
...

He has ded
... service and
but, unable to go
... penniless. An
... in which
... of gold
... of the tim
Bonaparte. This
... a burden to
from hiding-place
... occasional sev
... to be wonder
the whole village
German 577

Mr Arthur gives
the clever awaken
people to their
Osborne's first
boys' ... firing
the fish set to
...

Canada Blackie
and Prison Reform

Mr. Osborne's Methods an Enemy of Society

Canada Blackie died recently at Sing Sing, a star exhibit of
the results of Mr. Osborne's prison methods. As a boy the
prisoner ran away from home and joined a circus, which he
deserted after causing an accident that crippled one of the
performers (a woman) for life. He became the head of a band
of yeggmen, and served a term in Joliet prison in the old days
of straitjackets, hanging by the wrists, and other methods of
discipline. He emerged from the penitentiary a confirmed
enemy of society, took part in a safe robbery in which a
watchman was killed, and received a life sentence, which he
began at Dannemora. Here, for seven years, his record was
unexceptionable, "but the iron and stone enters his very
soul and his nerves were shattered by the thousand and one
petty rules and humiliations of the stupid system." So, by
the underground system of convicts, he obtained enough
dynamite to blow up the north end of the prison block, but
was betrayed by a stool pigeon. Solitary confinement was
the cost.

In his dark cell the man obtained in a still more mysterious manner a piece of gas pipe, which he fashioned into a revolver, making the charge from the heads of matches and the sides of matchboxes. With this weapon he shot a guard through the shoulder, the result being an additional sentence of ten years. Altogether, he spent twenty months in the dark cell. Finally he was transferred to Auburn, blind in one eye and a victim of tuberculosis. Here he met Donald Lowrie, the author of *My Life in Prison* and *My Life Out of Prison*, and came under Mr. Osborne's influence.

This is the story told in this book. It is mostly made up, however, of Blackie's letters to the Warden, to Donald Lowrie, and others. Of the rebellious, indomitable criminal there is not a trace left in these epistles. One wonders, as a matter of fact, how much of the man's conversion, of his immediate surrender, was due to the debilitating progress of his disease and how much to the changed methods of prison governance. Some of these letters are, indeed, almost too sweet; a few passages in them — to Mr. Osborne, Mr. Whitman, and the director of the Connecticut Reformatory at Cheshire — are almost patronizingly encouraging: "Go to it, dear friend. You can win the confidence of the fellows. I know it. You won everyone here. I do not wish to flatter you, Mr. Hubbard, but I am going to be frank. You have made a lasting impression with the boys. I tell you, you can win out. It's not flattery as I said, but honest stuff." Again, to Mr. Whitman, during his campaign for Governorship: "I stood directly underneath you while you were speaking [in the prison yard at Auburn]. And I am pleased very much to state that the look in your eyes was sincere as the ring in your voice. We, of course, felt that we wanted a man at Albany who would be with us, and we felt that you might be that man. But now——." Blackie died happy, a pardoned man, and the star exhibit of Mr. Osborne's reform methods.

New-York Tribune
September 3, 1915

The Story of "Canada Blackie"

by
Thomas Mott Osborne
Warden of Sing Sing

The Story of "Canada Blackie"

By Thomas Mott Osborne

Warden of Sing Sing

(An address before the members of the Republican Club, New York City.)

When I accepted the invitation to be here this afternoon, although I could be here but a very short time, it was with the understanding, on my part, at least, that I was to listen and not to speak, but when I got here I found my name on the program, and even though I shall have to commit the sin, the discourteous sin, of running away after I have spoken, still I have allowed myself to be prevailed upon to say a few words. I do so the more readily because what I have to say is really but to give a concrete example of the work of Dr. Greer's discourse. And so, without any preface, I am going to plunge at once into my story. I will tell you one or two incidents.

Many of you may have seen in the newspapers a brief notice within the past week of the death, just a week ago this morning, of John E. Murphy, better known as _____, who died in the _____ home in _____ City a week ago to-day. I think a very brief story of Blackie's career will be interesting. In spite of his name he was not a negro, but a Californian of dark complexion, with hair and very piercing black eyes. Some twenty-five years ago, before he was fifteen years of age, he was a resident of Joliet Prison in the State of Illinois, and he bore on his wrists the marks of handcuffs when he was strung up with his hands tied behind his back, with his toes just touching the ground, as a punishment in that institution. He said to me, somewhat _____, a few days before his death, that had he been treated fairly the first time he got into prison, his story might have been different. The fact of the matter was, he developed into an outlaw of singular boldness and ability.

Thirteen years ago in this State he was concerned in a bank robbery where the watchman was killed. Two men went to the electric chair for that death, and Blackie was sentenced to life imprisonment. For several years confined in the prison at Dannemora, he was a model prisoner. Most thinking men are model prisoners. That is one of the evils of the prison system. Then, whether his story is accurate, there a slight difference of opinion between him and the doctor produced constant nagging until his nerves gave out, or whether his nerves gave out on account of the general prison system, makes very little difference. The fact of the matter was they did give out and that he got into constant trouble, and determined to make a bold dash for liberty. Together with three other men and armed with a pistol which he had manufactured out of a piece of gas pipe, and getting the explosives from match heads, they succeeded in getting as far as the warden's office, barricading themselves and wounding one of the guards who still bears a crippled arm. The four men were overcome, however, and taken down to Plattsburg, where the present Superintendent of Prisons, then the county judge, sentenced him to an additional ten years. When I first met Blackie I asked him what his term was—how long—and he said, "Life and ten years," and when he saw my mouth twitching a little at the reply, he added, "It does seem a little superfluous, doesn't it?" Coming back to Dannemora, he was put not only in solitary confinement, but in the dark cell for one year and eight months, lying on the stone floor and contracting the disease of which he died last week. After that, of course, the only resource—mental resource—he had was what he could find within himself. He counted the pin-holes in his door, he pulled off the buttons of his coat and used up some time by getting as far

as he could and throwing them over his shoulder and seeing how long it would take him to find them all. Then after he came out of the dark cell he was considered the most dangerous criminal in the State of New York, as he indeed very well was. He was so dangerous that they didn't dare keep him in Dannemora because of danger of his making trouble through the prison, and, even in the dark cell they couldn't keep him permanently from reaching the fellow prisoners. He was removed to _____ and placed in solitary confinement. When Warden _____ began saying freedom to the prisoners in the State of _____ _____ prison reform came in and I often asked myself whether the thing really better was his interest _____

_____ he said that _____ dangerous _____

Next day I brought Blackie into the yard, and one of the most _____ things I have ever witnessed was this every _____ who, after two years in solitary confinement, came out since he was dropped in the prison. The attitude of these assembled prisoners was that of hero-worship. You could see he was a hero in the eyes of these men. The next month he was elected one of the board of delegates of the Mutual Welfare League and was promptly elected one of the executive board, receiving the highest number of votes of any candidate. By September he was one of the most trusted prisoners of the Auburn prison. He was brought to Sing Sing in September in the hopes that the climate might benefit him. He was acting and thinking day and night as to how he could benefit his fellow prisoners. He called one of the prisoners up to his room, and said to him, "Now, I want you to understand the new order of things. I want you to realize that this is no longer the old system. You were accustomed to buck against the old system, but you never would squeal on your pals. In this new system you must understand that the warden is your pal," and so his tremendous influence—perhaps the largest influence in the prisons of any man in the State of New York—was continually exercised to bring about right acting of prisoners toward the authorities, and to help forward the reign of liberty and order under self-governing principles.

But the disease which had fastened on him in the dark cells at Dannemora proved too strong, and he died a week ago to-day.

Now, gentlemen, which is the right spirit? Which is according to the American ideals? Which is according to the dictates of common sense? The system which brings about

The Story of "Canada Blackie"

An address before the members of the Republican Club, New York City.

When I accepted the invitation to be here this afternoon, although I could be here but a very short time, it was with the understanding, on my part, at least, that I was to listen and not to speak, but when I got here I found my name on the program, and even though I shall have to commit the sin, the discourteous sin, of running away after I have spoken, still I have allowed myself to be prevailed upon to say a few words. I do so the more readily because what I have to say is really but to give a concrete example of the spirit of Dr. Greer's discourse. And so, without any preface, I am going to plunge at once into my story. I will tell you one or two incidents.

Many of you may have seen in the newspapers a brief notice within the past week of the death, just a week ago this morning, of John E. Murphy, better known as "Canada Blackie," who died in the warden's house in Sing Sing a week ago today. I think a very brief story of Blackie's career will be interesting. In spite of his name, he was not a negro, but a Californian of dark complexion, black hair, and very piercing black eyes. Some twenty-five years ago, before he was twenty years of age, he was a resident of Joliet Prison in the State of Illinois, and he bore on his wrists the marks of handcuffs when he was strung up with his hands tied behind his back, with his toes just touching the ground, as a punishment while in that institution. He said to me, somewhat pathetically, a few days before his death, that had he been treated fairly that first time he got into prison, his story might have been different. The fact of the matter was, he developed into an outlaw of singular boldness and ability.

Thirteen years ago in this State he was concerned in a bank robbery where the watchman was killed. Two men went to the electric chair for that death, and Blackie was sentenced to life imprisonment. For seven years confined in the prison at Dannemora, he was a model prisoner. Most third-termers are model prisoners. That is one of the evils of the prison system. Then, whether his story is accurate, that a slight difference of opinion between him and the doctor produced constant nagging until his nerves gave out, or whether his nerves gave out on account of the general prison system, makes very little difference. The fact of the matter was they did give out and that he got into constant trouble, and determined to make a bold dash for liberty. Together with three other men and armed with a pistol which he had manufactured out of a piece of gas pipe, and getting the explosives from match heads, they succeeded in getting as far as the warden's office, barricading themselves and wounding one of the guards who still bears a crippled arm. The four men were overcome, however, and taken down to Plattsburg, where the present Superintendent of Prisons, then the county judge,[1] sentenced him to an additional ten years. When I first met Blackie I asked him what his term was — how long — and he said, "Life and ten years," and when he saw my mouth twitching a little at the reply, he added, "It does seem a little superfluous, doesn't it?" Coming back to Dannemora, he was put not only in solitary confinement, but in the dark cell

[1] John B. Riley (pp. 2, 6)

for one year and eight months, lying on the stone floor and contracting the disease of which he died last week. After that, of course, the only resource — mental resource — he had was what he could find within himself. He counted the pinholes in his door, he pulled off the buttons of his coat and used up some time by getting as far as he could and throwing them over his shoulder and seeing how long it would take him to find them all. Then after he came out of the dark cell he was considered the most dangerous criminal in the State of New York, as he might very well be. He was so dangerous they didn't dare keep him in Dannemora because of the rumors of dynamite hidden around the prison yard, and even in the dark cell they couldn't keep his personality from reaching his fellow prisoners. He was removed to Auburn and placed in solitary confinement. When Warden Rattigan began giving freedom to the prisoners in the State of New York, Blackie was very much interested, as he had been interested in the plans for prison reform that he and I often talked of before the thing really began, and his interest and his feeling became so strong that after the first day that the men spent out in the yard, the 30th of last May, Blackie took me into his cell one afternoon and said, "I have something here I want you to give to the warden." Mind you, up to this time he was still considered so dangerous that when he requested to be brought up to the warden's room for an interview with me — he was even suspicious of the officials — the warden refused to let him come. He said, "I don't dare to do it because I don't want to take the responsibility of what might happen." I went into his cell. He reached for a can of talcum powder, hollowed out a little hole in the powder and presented me with a key which fitted the lock of his cell. Reaching through the bars, he could unlock his cell at any moment. Then he reached out a steel knife saying, "There isn't another man in prison that could have made that." When he handed me the knife he said, "I intended to use that, but I feel so deeply what Warden Rattigan and you are trying to do for the prisoners

ch. ends p. 124

that I decided to give it to you. Tell the warden he need not have any anxiety here, because I am going straight."

Next day I brought Blackie out into the yard, and one of the most dramatic scenes I have ever witnessed was this event — this man after five years in solitary confinement, twelve years since he had stepped on the grass. The attitude of the other prisoners toward him was that of hero-worship. You could see that he was a hero in the eyes of those men. The next month he was elected one of the board of delegates of the Mutual Welfare League, and was promptly elected one of the executive board, receiving the highest number of votes of any candidate. By September he was one of the most trusted prisoners of the Auburn prison. He was brought to Sing Sing in September[2] in the hopes that the climate might benefit him. He was acting and thinking day and night as to how he could benefit his fellow prisoners. He called one of the prisoners up to his room, and said to him, "Now, I want you to understand the new order of things. I want you to realize that this is no longer the old system. You were accustomed to buck against the old system, but you never would squeal on your pals. In this new system you must understand that the warden is your pal," and so his tremendous influence — perhaps the largest influence in the prisons of any man in the State of New York, was continually exercised to bring about right acting of prisoners toward the authorities, and to help forward the reign of liberty and order under self-governing principles.

But the disease which had fastened on him in the dark cells at Dannemora proved too strong, and he died a week ago today.

Now, gentlemen, which is the right spirit? Which is according to the American ideals? Which is according to the dictates of common sense? The system which brings about the dangerous animal known as "Canada Blackie" or the one which brings that man into line with the forces of

[2] Actual date: December 31, 1914 (p. 53). Confirmed by prison transfer records.

righteousness in society, inside and outside the prison? If you are a regular reader of the newspapers, you have seen a good deal about what we are doing up at Sing Sing, and as usual, the newspapers touch for the most part only the superficial aspect of it. I beg you to believe that the superficial aspect is only superficial; that down at the bottom we have a consistent policy, not of giving moving picture shows to prisoners, although the witnessing of picture shows is far better than keeping them locked up in their cells contracting tuberculosis. Moving picture shows are not the aim, not the end; the baseball games are not the end; they are only means of restoring to these men their equilibrium, because I believe that my job is to try and send those men back into the world better adapted to lead honest and capable lives than when they came in.

Now, one more story. You have heard a great deal about the "dope" question at Sing Sing, and everyone knows the contracting of the drug habit has been the curse of Sing Sing.

Do you know why they have contracted that habit?

To forget the horrible Sunday afternoons; because the way they celebrated the Lord's Day was by being locked in their cells all day long — for more than twenty hours shut up in those damp, deadly cells. Now, then, there was the most difficult problem that I had to face. How did I handle it? By doing nothing at all, because I left it to the end. What has happened? It has taken care of itself. Because the men trusted and given responsibility for it, have practically wiped the drugs out of Sing Sing themselves. To me it has been the most amazing thing in all my experience in life, but I know what I tell you is true. In January a man came to me. He was a wreck. He was just out of a hospital, having taken a cure for the drug. He had a wife and three children. He wanted to get away from the habit. I asked him, "Have you ever been in prison before?"

"Eleven times."

Said I, "I hope you will have the strength to win."

ch. ends next p.

He said, "I will try, but I don't know — one of the 'screws' wants my watch."

He meant one of the officers, because some of the officers peddled drugs inside the prison. And two days afterward I was met by a man who said as he passed, "The watch is gone," and not knowing how to tackle the problem, still I did nothing, and about three weeks ago I met at the foot of the stairs a man. He stood up straight, six feet high, broad shoulders. I said, "Good gracious, I didn't recognize you."

"Mr. Osborne, I have gained forty pounds."

Said I, "It isn't possible!"

"I don't believe there is an once of 'dope' in the place. If you can get it, I don't know how to get it, and I could get it if anybody could. I have got my watch."

Said I, "How?"

"The 'screw' brought it back to me, saying as he did so, 'The warden didn't ask any questions, but December 1 is coming, and I think I had better go on the level.'"

Since that time I have found, not from one source, but from two or three, that there is very little drug-taking in Sing Sing today. Perhaps you will believe that I am not exaggerating the lessening of the drug-evil at the prison if I tell you that two of the prisoners recently held up the guard who was bringing the stuff into the jail and made him destroy it. That is what will happen when you treat men according to American ideals, when you give them responsibility, when you treat them like men. One poet has spoken about the English people as those who "Forever they are dreamers who make the dream come true."[3] We are taught to be a very practical people. Well, we are in some ways, but thank heaven, we are not altogether practical. We are not altogether pursuing the dollar. We have our dreams now up there at Sing Sing. I had a dream that we could take these mournful wrecks and turn them out men, and the dream is coming true.

---

[3] Stanza 20, Line 6 of *Ode on the Coronation of King Edward* (June 1902) by Canadian poet William Bliss Carman (1861–1929).

Heathenry:
Coda

The Fact of Canada Blackie

Here's what we know—or don't:

John E. Murphy, alias Canada Blackie, alias John Hamilton, age 42, died at 7:10 a.m. Saturday, March 20, 1915, on the third floor of the warden's residence at Sing Sing.

No actual date of birth has yet presented itself, but we can assume 1873–74. Sing Sing states Buffalo, New York, as his place of birth, but the Auburn registry says Canada under Nativity, then Mrs. Field confirms "Canada" by birth, and Osborne called him both a Canadian and a Californian.

At the time of his last arrest Sing Sing states place of residence as Hamilton, Canada.

He had a mother of refinement that died when he was young and an unsympathetic father of intelligence who chose brutality when drunk — explanations, both, for his running away and becoming a circus trapeze artist for two years until, distracted, he failed to catch his partner (in the days before safety nets) which promptly ended both careers.

Next, he was a cowboy, then a train bandit.

He had one sister.

He served at least 30 days (possibly more) in an Illinois prison, likely Joliet, in 1892, age 19; then five days (possibly more) in Albany, age 26, 1899. We're not certain, but the Sing Sing registry appears to list the offense in both cases as "drunk" (see right), which jibes with his answer of "intemp" (short for intemperate, or lack of moderation) to the question of "habits" (liquor use), which jibes with the note under Remarks on his Sing Sing Statement of Commitments: "30 Days + 5 Days in jail Intoxications."

He was a natural, charismatic leader and his mother thought he should be a priest.

He "never could stand stupidity in anything" and pinpoints his first jolt as a teenager in Joliet with setting his lawless streak ablaze, "I knew no authority, and took pride in recklessness. The greatest sensation I ever had was standing with a loaded revolver over an engineer's heart, and ordering him to slow down an express train for *me!*"

At some point during these early exploits he spent "a night and a day in the woods with a bullet hole through his jaw."

He was known to have a keen sense of humor, which may explain why one registry says Occupation: Marble Polisher and another says Fireman.

He was a single, tobacco-using Catholic with large burn scars on the back of one forearm and tattoos on the front of each — one a sailor, a girl, and a flag; the other an "American coat of arms."

He stood 5'9½" tall, weighed 140 pounds, and wore a medium complexion with piercing, deep-set brown eyes supporting "arched and good high brows," with a full head of dark hair mixed gray under a 7 hat, atop 8 shoes.

"Teeth good" says registry, then: one gold-filled upper front tooth over one lower gold crown.

And he could read and write.[1]

On the evening of Monday, November 26, 1900, night watchman Matthew Wilson was patrolling his beat when he observed six strangers in Cobleskill, New York, and advised a citizen that he was going home to get his revolver.

---

[1] All per Blackie's Clinton, Auburn, and Sing Sing registry entries at right.

6040 John Murphy | Schoharie | Murder 2d | Supreme

32378 John Murphy | Schoharie Supreme Cochrane Jacy | Filed Jury Assault 1st Deg

32378 John Murphy " 19 " Murder 1st

55617 Murphy, John Schoharie Murder 2nd Supreme Cochrane " 13, 1903

Otsego Ill Jail 1892. Drunk 30 Days
Albany " 1899 - " 5 "

John Murphy (Discharged by Pardon Feby 20/15)

No. 55617
Clinton No. 6040

Received from Schoharie County Supreme Court. At Clinton Prison April 17, 1903
Sentenced, April 13, 1903 Life Con Murder 2nd Hon. A. V. S. Cochrane, Judge,
Who arrested you? Det. Chief Kane & O'Connor at Buffalo N.Y. Precinct No.
Born, Buffalo N.Y. Age, 31 Occupation Marble Polisher
Complexion, Med, Eyes, Brown Hair Dk Hair mixed with gray.
Stature, 5 — 9½ Weight, 140 Read, Yes Write Yes
Habits, Intemp Tobacco, Yes Religion Cath Married or Single,
Resided when Arrested, at Hamilton Canada.
Names of Relatives or Friends. Friend Mrs A. Baldwin Blenheim Schoharie Co. N.Y.
Med head — 7 Hat. 8 Shoes. Med. ears. Small scar Sr ear. Arched and good left brows. Rather Deep Set Eyes. Teeth good. One gold crown lower front & one gold filled upper front tooth. Tat Sailor & girl & flag & C on front Sr forearm and Large Scars from burns back of same arm. Tat American Coat of arms on front of Sr Forearm.
(Died at 7:10 A.M. March 20, 1915 in wardens House)

1905 Received from Clinton late May 6, 1905 + Put on Count 5/8/05

30 Days & 5 Days in jail Dulpication.

---

p. 34
1905
Received from Clinton late
May 6, 1905 + Put on
count 5/8/05

No. 55617

Clinton No. 6040

Names of
Relatives or Friends

Ill. Jail 1892.   30 Days
Albany " 1899 - " 5 "

John Murphy (Discharged by Pardon Febry 20/15)
Canada Blackie
Received from Schoharie County Supreme Court. at Clinton Prison April 17, 1903
Sentenced, April 13, 1903 Life Cou Murder 2nd Hon. A. V. S. Cochrane Judge,
Who arrested you? Detective Kane O'Connor at Buffalo, NY Precinct No. ——
Born, Buffalo, NY Age, 31 Occupation, Marble Polisher
Complexion, Med. Eyes, Brown Hair, Dk Hair mixed with gray.
Stature, 5-9½ Weight, 140 Read, Yes Write, Yes
Habits, Intemp Tobacco, Yes Religion, Cath Married or Single,
Resided when Arrested, at Hamilton, Canada.
Friend Mrs A. Baldwin Blenheim Schoharie Co. NY
Med head — 7 hat, 8 shoes. Med
ears. Small scar across   ear. Arched and
good high brows. Rather deepset eyes
Teeth good. One gold crown lower front &
one gold filled upper front tooth. Tat Sailor
& girl & flag(s)   front   forearm and
Large scars from burns on back of same
arm. Tat American coat of arms on
front of   forearm.
(Died at 7:10 a.m. March 20, 1915 in warden's house)

Approximately 2 a.m., four men were seen coming down West Main Street and it is supposed Wilson came in contact with them at the corner of Main and Union Streets.[2]

Several shots were fired and at least four bullets penetrated plate glass windows in the stores opposite.

A moment later, Wilson's body was found lying face down on the steps of Martin B. Borst's grocery with four bullet holes in it. Beside him lay his revolver with five empty chambers. Five men were seen running toward the railroad tracks and disappeared in darkness.

A separate report says a gang of seven or eight were discovered that November occupying a railroad hut near Cobleskill. On the evening of the crime one of the gang was observed removing a clothesline from a house in the suburbs, which caught the eye of Wilson, who suspected that the rope was to be used in a burglary. This version introduces a separate bank watchman, who Wilson warned: "You keep quiet, and if they make any attempt, I'll shoot."

Then, just as two or three of the gang were about to break-and-enter the back door of the First National Bank, Wilson sprang onto the scene and O'Connor, alias O'Connell, alias Goat Hinch, fired a bullet that entered Wilson's brain.[3]

The gang escaped.

A third report says six men rode into town on a Delaware & Hudson freight train from Albany, and alighted before the train entered Cobleskill. Wilson became suspicious when he saw them approach the First National Bank and notified a restaurant keeper friend, arming him with a revolver, and instructing him to follow the men while he, Wilson, would go around the block to head them off.

The restaurant keeper did as instructed, but heard shots as he caught up with the men, then discovered Wilson dead.

The burglars disappeared.

All reports say a search of the area yielded a "number of

[2] Burglars Kill a Watchman. (1900, November 28). *The New York Times*, p. A10.
[3] He is a "Yeggs" and Tramp Thief: The Man with Many Aliases is Released from the Penitentiary. (1901, February 6) *The Brooklyn Citizen*, p. A11.

burglar's tools" around the back door and/or in the grass near the First National Bank. One report says the tools had been stolen from the local toolhouse of the Delaware and Hudson River Railroad Company.

In response to the attempted burglary, it was reported:

"The First National Bank of Cobleskill, N.Y., is a member of the American Bankers' Association, and as these men evidently intended to commit a burglary in the bank, the Bankers' Association instructed its detective agents, the Pinkertons, to spare no expense in determining the identity of the men and, if possible, to cause their arrest."[4]

Pinkerton Assistant Superintendent Dougherty took charge of the case.

Blackie, then age 27, was either the last of six[5] or one of nine[6] "Yegg" Gang members to be identified by Pinkertons and arrested by Detective Sergeant Cain O'Connor,[7] and maybe Detective Barrett, of Buffalo Precinct No. 3.

They were discovered when O'Connor and Barrett released an unnamed man on January 13, 1902, and tailed him straight to Yegg headquarters at No. 40 Oak Street.

On Tuesday, January 14, "a squad of patrolmen surrounded the house" and the detectives entered to find the gang playing cards in the basement. All were arrested and charged with vagrancy, initially, except one who escaped.

A search of the premises revealed dynamite fuses, cans of nitroglycerin, a dozen or more revolvers, and yegg clues like "an outfit such as is used by safe-blowers."

[4] The Chair for "Goat Hinch." (1902, January 26). *The Brooklyn Daily Eagle*, Fourth Section p. 12.

[5] "Last of 'Yegg' Gang: Canada Blackie to be Tried for Murder of Cobleskill Bank Watchman. (1902, February 8). *Democrat Chronicle*. p. A1.

[6] Bad Gang of Crooks: One of the Men Identified by Pinkertons as "Canada Blackie," Wanted for Murder. (1902, February 6) *The Buffalo Review*, p. A7.

[7] 'Big Ed' Kelly's Race About Run. (1906, March 25). *Buffalo Courier*, p. A1.

What's a yegg, exactly? The *San Francisco Call* inquired exactly that of Detective William A. Pinkerton:[8]

> ". . . the history of the yeggmen has been acquired during fifteen years' study of the fellows, made necessary by their frequent violations of the laws of the various States, including almost everything in the category of crime from murder and robbery down to assault and petty larceny. He has traced the origin of their name back to the gypsy bands of the European continent, who were in the habit of designating a clever thief among them as a 'yegg,' or head chief of the gang. Eventually, the American hobos bestowed the title of 'yegg' on the more daring thieves with whom they were wont to travel, and it finally came into use among the worst element of criminals that infest the country. In the opinion of Detective Pinkerton, and his wisdom is seldom questioned among the criminal hunters of the Western hemisphere, the most dangerous criminal abroad in the land today is the yeggman."

The Brooklyn Citizen published a simpler definition: "bank burglars who use nitroglycerine on safes, and prepare the compound themselves."

Depending on the source, other members of the Yegg Gang included:

- James Sullivan, alias Whitey Sullivan, alias James P., alias James Sutton, who was arrested in Syracuse March 25, 1901, as he was being released from the Onondaga County Jail. A jury returned a guilty verdict of murder first degree at 5:30 p.m. on October 25, 1901, and he was sentenced to death by Judge Chester two hours later.[9] The next day, a newspaper noted:

[8] Detective Pinkerton versus The Yeggman. (1905, December 3) *The San Francisco Call*, p. 5.

[9] Sullivan Must Die. (1901, October 27). *The Pittsburgh Press*, p. 4

"Sullivan's conviction was purely on circumstantial evidence."[10] He was granted a reprieve, twice, by Governor Odell — the first on November 22, 1901,[11] then again on February 24, 1902, so that new evidence could be presented to Judge Betts at Kingston.[12] On March 16, Judge Betts considered the evidence, but decided it was not sufficient to warrant a new trial. Sullivan was notified, then "walked steadily to the chair, protesting his innocence to the last"[13] and was electrocuted Monday, March 24, 1902. "It was said that he came from a good family in Ohio."

- William O'Connor, alias O'Connell, alias Montgomery, alias Hinch, alias Thomas Sullivan, alias Goat Hinch, alias The Goat — who previously served two years at the Illinois Reformatory, 1888–1890; one year at Joliet Prison beginning June 1890, then again in 1893; then three or five years at Trenton, New Jersey, starting 1895[14] — was arrested in Dobbs Ferry, New York, on January 3, 1901, and sentenced a day later to three months in Kings County Penitentiary on a charge of "vagrancy and suspicious character" "in order to give the authorities time to work up evidence against him."[15] He was released on a writ of *habeas corpus*[16] on February 6, and while celebrating the event in a saloon, No. 15 East Broadway, "he murdered Fred Chester, a negro piano player."[17]

[10] Sullivan is Guilty: Sentenced by Judge Chester to be Electrocuted During December. (1901, October 26). *Elmira Gazette*, p. A1.
[11] Slayer Sullivan Appeals. (1901, November 23). *The Sun* (Delaware), p. A3.
[12] Sullivan Pays Death Penalty. (1903, March 24). *The Evening World*, p. A7.
[13] Sullivan Dies Protesting: When Led to Electric Chair He Repeats That He is Innocent. (1903, March 25). *New York Tribune*, p. A6.
[14] Twice a Murderer: Man with Jersey City Record on Trial in New York. (1901, May 31). *The Jersey City News*, 13(3691), p. A1.
[15] Murder Warrant for O'Connell. (1901, January 5). *New-York Tribune*, p. A11.
[16] A writ ordering a prisoner to be brought before a judge to determine if they've been incarcerated illegally therefore requiring immediate release.
[17] His Two Roads to Death Chair: Goat Hinch Accussed of Two Murders Far Apart. (1901, May 31). *The Evening World*, p. A12.

Arrest and indictment followed. He was temporarily discharged by Justice Fursman, in the Criminal Branch of the Supreme Court on May 31, so that he could be brought to trial in Cobleskill for Wilson's murder, with the understanding "in case he is not convicted there he will be brought back to stand trial on the other charge." His trial began on January, 21, 1902, with Judge D. Cady Herrick of Albany presiding. Attorney George M. Palmer conducted the prosecution, while Hinch was defended by S. L. & C. B. Mayhem.[18] He was sentenced on January 25, for murder first degree, then electrocuted at Dannemora, alias Clinton on Tuesday, July 7, 1903, at either 10:18 or 11:38 a.m. "A minute later he was pronounced dead."

- Edward Jackson, alias Dublin Ned, alias Frank Ward, age 42, of Boston, who was arrested at 59th Street and Columbus Avenue, New York,[19] on December 19 or 20, 1901, and pled guilty on January 25, 1902,[20] to either burglary or attempted and confessed to being present during the Wilson debacle but took no part in the shooting. He was sentenced to nine years and eleven months at Clinton, alias Dannemora, and agreed to testify for the state at Blackie's trial.

- William Harris, alias Sheeny Harris, alias William Farley, who was arrested on a prior[21] at Little Falls, New York, Sunday, March 17, 1901, then turned state's evidence and confessed he and Dublin Ned were waiting on another corner when the Wilson shooting occurred, and "it was on his testimony, corroborated," that Sullivan and Hinch were electrocuted.

---

[18] Trial of "Goat" Hinch for First Degree Murder. (1902, January 21). *Elmira Gazette*, 58(17), p. A1.

[19] Arrest Recalls Bank Tragedy. (1901, December 21). *The Evening World*, p. A8.

[20] "Goat" Hinch Guilty. (1902, January 26). *The Sun*, p. A12.

[21] Well Known Crook Arrested. (1901, March 18). *Asbury Park Press*, p. A4.

- **Charles Foulke**, alias Folk, alias Voulks, alias Ballard, alias Charlie, who was killed in an explosion while attempting to crack a safe in Norfolk or Richmond, Virginia, near Washington D.C., February 1901. One report says: "He had a quantity of nitroglycerine, but being an amateur caused a premature explosion, which blew him to pieces."[22]

One paper says this Yegg Gang of 6 left Albany on the night of the crime and while en route to Stamford, New York, it was decided to stop off at Cobleskill and rob the First National Bank.[23]

Another paper says nine total were arrested, including:

- **David Martin**, alias Frank Mason, alias Crock, also wanted in connection with a local bank and post office robbery.

A third paper says they were all pals of Ed Kelley, alias Howard, alias Graham, and "known to the yeggmen with whom he travels as Big Ed."

This time, including Blackie, there are seven:

- John Grant
- Frank Hatch
- Joseph Bigardi
- Thomas Crane
- John Cunningham
- Dave Martin

It goes on to say that the inspector believed there was "sufficient evidence to connect them with several post office robberies which have occurred throughout the western part of the state during the past year."

[22] "Dublin Ned" Arrested. (1901, December 22). *The Boston Globe*, p. A2.
[23] William O'Connor was Legally Killed Today. (1903, July 7). *Elmira Daily Gazette*, p. A1

Then: "A particular effort has been made to connect them with the robbery of the post office of Brockton on Thanksgiving Eve."

Ending with: "It is understood that they will be arrested on this latter charge upon release from the penitentiary on February 13. Several people at Brockton saw the men about the town on the day of the robbery and it is believed that they will be better able to identify them when released from the penitentiary and in ordinary street dress than when in prison garb."

Blackie was transferred from Erie County Penitentiary, Buffalo, to the Schoharie County Jail on Tuesday, February 7, 1902, to await trial.

After first pleading not guilty to one count murder first degree, he pled guilty to one count murder second degree and was sentenced to life imprisonment by Judge A. V. S. Cochrane in Schoharie County Supreme Court on Monday, April 13, 1903.

On Friday, April 17, he was transferred to Clinton Prison, alias Dannemora — No. 6040.

Nine days later, the Sunday edition of *The Sun* ran an article entitled: "Innocent Man Put to Death?"[24]

Wherein we meet Father James Curry, rector of St. James' Church, No. 23 Oliver Street, who had in his possession an affidavit to a statement made by Sheeny Harris that Whitey Sullivan died an innocent man.

The statement, which had been "kept secret" until Blackie's trial, was allegedly made on Monday, March 24, 1902, the day Sullivan was executed, and was sworn to by Mrs. Alice I. Baldwin, wife of the Schoharie County Sheriff, to whom Harris made the assertion after requesting an audience.

Harris was excited and trembling and spoke quickly, "I suppose Sullivan is dead, and he died an innocent man."

[24] Innocent Man Put to Death? Father Curry Says "Whitey" Sullivan Wasn't Guilty. (1903, April 26). *The Sun*, p. A9.

SULLIVAN PAYS DEATH PENALTY

The Man Whom Father Curry Tried to Save Dies To-Day in the Electric Chair in Clinton Prison.

KILLED A NIGHT WATCHMAN.

Priest Believed He Was Unjustly Convicted and Secured Two Reprieves from Gov. Odell, but Courts Confirmed the Sentence.

"GOAT HINCH" ELECTROCUTED

DANNEMORA, N. Y., July 7.—Wm. O'Connor, alias "Goat Hinch", was electrocuted here this morning at 10:10 for the murder of Matthew Wilson, a night watchman at Cobleskill, N. Y., in November, 1900.

The current was turned on at 10:15 a. m. and a minute later he was pronounced dead.

O'Connor is the second to suffer the death penalty for the murder of night watchman Wilson, of Cobleskill, on the evening of November 28, 1900. James P. alias "Whitey" Sullivan was electrocuted at Dannemora March 24 last, after having been twice reprieved by Governor Odell.

Sullivan, O'Connor, John Murphy, alias "Canada Blackie", Wm. Farley, alias "Sheeny Harris", Dublin Ned and Charles Ballard left Albany on the night of the crime for Stamford, N. Y. One the way it was proposed to stop off at Cobleskill and rob the First National Bank. The gang was successful and in an exchange of shots Wilson was killed. The gang was subsequently arrested except Ballar, who was later killed at Norfolk, Va.

Dublin Ned, who testified for the State, got off with nine years in Clinton prison. "Canada Blackie" was sentenced to the same prison for life a few months ago.

"Sheeny" Harris is still in jail at Schoharie awaiting trial.

PRISON FOR LIFE.

JOHN MURPHY, ALIAS CANADA BLACKIE, IS SENTENCED FOR MURDER.

Amsterdam, N. Y., April 18.—In the supreme court, at Schoharie, John Murphy, alias, Canada Blackie, who was to stand trial this week, and withdrew his former plea of not guilty of murder in the first degree and pleaded guilty to the second degree charge, whereupon Justice Cochrane sentenced him to life imprisonment in Clinton prison at hard labor. Murphy was implicated in the murder of a night watchman at Cobleskill, for which "Whitey" Sullivan was recently electrocuted.

JUDGE A. V. S. COCHRANE

He then said Sullivan and "Billy" (another alias for Blackie) were innocent of the crime and naturally were good men at heart. All he would say against them was that they would get drunk and get into bad company sometimes[25] — which jibes.

When asked if the affidavit named the real murderer Father Curry replied, "No, the statement was made by Harris, and he wouldn't implicate himself."

"You think, then, that Harris is the murderer?"

"Think so? I know it — that is, I have been so informed."

Father Curry refused to disclose the source of his information, but stated the District Attorney picked Sullivan as the particular member of the gang to be convicted, and that Curry's efforts to secure justice for Sullivan were hindered wherever possible. While he was trying to secure a new trial for Sullivan, he says he was twice told by two prominent men at Albany that he was "making an ass of himself," as Sullivan had confessed. Governor Odell denied the statement immediately afterward.

Father Curry also alleged Harris received undue favors for turning state's evidence and was taken from the jail and allowed to "be at liberty with a dissolute woman" one night, and deliberately perjured himself at the beginning of the trial by swearing that he was not an ex-convict and no notice was taken of his perjury even when a motion for a new trial was under consideration. If he perjured himself in this respect, it was argued, his entire testimony was worthless. Additional evidence[26] included an alibi provided by George Arden and Harry Hamlin who say they saw Sullivan in a saloon in Albany, 40 miles away, an hour before the murder — and statements from James J. O'Reilly and Edward J. Murphy, of Albany, who had also heard Harris confess that he had killed Wilson himself. Father Curry went on to say:

[25] Makes Affidavit Public: Sheriff Wife Tells How "Sheeny" Harris Absolved "Whitey" Sullivan of Guilt. (1903, April 27). *New-York Tribune*, p. A4.
[26] Plea for "Whitey" Sullivan. (1903, March 8). *The Sun*, p. A10.

"I am preparing a statement of the facts in this case that will prove startling when it is ready to be given out. I can't help poor Sullivan now, but what has come to me since he was executed will help at least clear his name of the crime of murder, no matter what else was against it. Besides doing this I will take the opportunity to show how certain people tried to deaden my interest in the case; how they tried to thwart my efforts to save Sullivan from his ignominious end.

"The first inkling I got of how the prosecution in this case stood was when 'Canada Blackie' (John Murphy) came up for trial for his part in the killing of the Cobleskill bank watchman. Clyde Propa, attorney for the defendant, was informed by Blackie that advances had been made to him that a plea of guilty of murder in the second degree would be accepted. The State's attorneys had heard of the affidavit made by Mrs. Baldwin, which Propa had intended to introduce as an impeachment of Harris' testimony should he be put on the witness stand against him. They did not relish such a thing.

"There were other things that would have been brought out, too. It would have been shown what favors had been shown Harris for his convenient testimony in the case, especially with reference to a certain night he was taken out of the Schoharie Jail to permit him to indulge in an orgie."[27]

Father Curry proceeds to name names in an article published by the *San Francisco Call* two days later:[28]

---

[27] Innocent, He is Executed: Father Curry Declares "Whitey" Sullivan was Electrocuted for a Crime He Did Not Commit. (1903, April 25). *The Evening World*, p. A5.

[28] Law Takes Life of Man Not Guilty: Proof of Innocence of Convict Executed in New York. (1903, April 27). *San Francisco Call*, p. A7.

ch. ends p. 142

"All I can do now is to prove Sullivan innocent. All I wanted was a stay of one week, but I could not get it because a certain State Senator was anxious to get Sullivan out of the way of Prosecutor Palmer's political future.

"Governor Odell was very kind to me, but as soon as I would leave him this State Senator would undo all the progress I had made. Why, at Albany people tried a hundred different ways to discourage me. They told me Sullivan had confessed. They told me they had seven or eight witnesses to prove his guilt, and they told the same thing to Governor Odell. I simply asked for time to present evidence which I was convinced would result in a new trial, but they influenced the Governor not to grant another stay."

On May 8, 1903, Blackie was transferred to Auburn — No. 32378.

On September 8, about a month before his scheduled trial, several papers reported that at 6:30 a.m. it was discovered that Sheeny Harris and two other prisoners had escaped overnight from the newly built, "escape proof" building at Schoharie County Jail by digging through a two-foot wall, "taking out more than a wagonload of masonry."[29]

On October 23, one of the men Sheeny escaped with was captured and confessed Sheeny was in New York City, headquartered in a saloon owned by an Italian.[30]

On May 6, 1905, Blackie was transferred to Sing Sing and put on the count May 8 — No. 55617.

Then, any news of the Yegg Gang goes quiet for a while.

Two irregularities in this timeline, however, has us perplexed due to Blackie's on-the-record transfers to Auburn in 1903, then Sing Sing in 1905, which contradict Blackie's

---

[29] "Sheenie" Harris Escapes: He and Two Others Dig Out of Schoharie County Jail. (1903, September 8). *The Sun*, 71(8), p. A1.

[30] Says "Sheeny" Harris is Here. (1903, October 25). *The Sun*, p. A3.

"story" that has him at Clinton, patiently doing time, until the dynamite-in-the-prison-yard episode. At the time of this writing, we are unable to locate any record of a transfer from Sing Sing back to Clinton prior to that fiasco, which isn't to say that it doesn't exist or that the records are incorrect.

Regardless, on October 23, 1909, the Associated Press syndicated a story that on the previous evening, October 22, six convicts were apprehended just prior to attempting an explosive escape from Clinton "armed with a loaded revolver and two sticks of dynamite." The plot was foiled when a lifer with a clean record ratted them out to Warden Cole, who reported it to Superintendent Collins. Those implicated in addition to Blackie included Harry Miller, a yegg from New York, and Big Ed Kelley, serving a life sentence for murder. The recovered revolver belonged to a prison guard and had mysteriously disappeared the previous November, and it was speculated that the dynamite was secured from a group of convicts that had recently been engaged in constructing a road near the prison.[31]

On June 16, 1910, *The Washington Herald* reported the capture of William Schafer, alias Sheeny Harris, in Towson, Maryland, on a burglary charge, and notes after his escape from the Schoharie County Jail in 1903 he "went to Europe, where he has been until recently."[32]

On October 6, 1911, *The Sun* ran an article[33] detailing how the appointment of Col. Joseph H. Scott as State Super-intendent of Prisons and his ordering of careful investigation of every prison under his jurisdiction brought to light the assertion that discipline at Clinton had been slack for several years. It goes on to list (but not date) several incidents

[31] Desperate Aim of Six Convicts in Attempt to Escape from the Clinton Jail. (1909, October 23). *The Evening Citizen* (Ottawa), p. A18.

[32] Admits Theft and Murder: Prisoner Who Turned State's Evidence Says He Escaped Before Trial. (1910, June 16). *The Washington Post*, p. A12.

[33] Tunnel at Clinton Prison was Nearly Finished for Big Jail Delivery. (1911, October 6). *The Sun*, p. A2.

that had occurred at the prison to illustrate the assertion, including:

" . . . three desperate convicts, Minfield, Curtis, and John Murphy, alias Canada Blackie, made a raid with homemade pistols constructed of gas pipe on the administration department where Guard Healy found them in the correspondence department. Murphy shot Healy, tearing part of his hand away. Though painfully wounded, Healy kept his nerve and with his remaining hand covered the convicts with a revolver and marched them to the guard room."

For this act, Blackie was convicted of assault first degree by Judge John B. Riley[34] on May 14, 1912, and sentenced to an additional ten years "to begin at the expiration of his present sentence."

Blackie, now labeled as the "most notorious criminal in New York state," was transferred to Auburn on July 19, 1912, and sent directly to solitary where it was assumed by all that he would live out the rest of his days.

But then, in May 1913, a tall gentleman, age 53, stuck his hand through the bars of Blackie's cell door and proffered a handshake — that man was Thomas Mott Osborne. That chance meeting would forever alter the trajectory of the rest of Blackie's short life.

On September 29, Osborne entered Auburn to serve as voluntary prisoner "Tom Brown" for one week.

In April 1914, Donald Lowrie, at the invitation of Warden Rattigan and with Billy Duffy as guide, met Blackie for the first time in solitary at Auburn.

On June 2, 1914, Blackie fully committed himself to Osborne's "new penology" by inviting Osborne to his cell and handing over the cell key and a knife which he had crafted by hand.

---

[34] Riley succeeded Col. Scott as State Superintendent of Prisons in 1913.

The following day, June 3, 1914, Osborne, after convincing Warden Rattigan of Blackie's sincerity to make good, escorted Blackie to the prison yard at Auburn. It was the first time in nearly two years that Blackie had felt the warm sun upon his skin and breathed clean fresh air.

Then, on a Sunday in early October 1914, Blackie nearly fainted when his eyes suddenly met those of Mrs. Anne Porter Lynes Field for the first time. So much like his own mother did she look that he swore he was seeing a ghost. Needless to say that if that destined moment had never occurred, then you would not, now, be reading these words.

Then due to his rapidly declining health, Blackie was transferred from Auburn to Sing Sing on December 31, 1914, where it was hoped a change in climate would aid in his recovery, but the move would prove futile.

Once Blackie's grim prognosis was wholly clear and his end was drawing near, Governor Charles Whitman reluctantly agreed to a pardon on February 16, 1915.

Four days later, on February 20, 1915, Blackie was officially discharged from Sing Sing by pardon, but was too weak to leave prison, so Osborne, then warden of Sing Sing, allowed him to continue his residence on the third floor of the warden's house.

It was there that John E. Murphy passed away at 7:10 a.m. on March 20, 1915.

Soon after, in honor of the reformed criminal's life, a full-page article (also reprinting Blackie's first letter to Lowrie) was syndicated in newspapers. On May 16, 1915, *The Minneapolis Journal* published their version featuring something not seen in any other paper: a note from John F. McCarthy, alias John Otto Dandrell, alias Philadelphia Johnny, alias West Philadelphia Johnny,[35] a former bank robber:

---

[35] Struggling Back to Their Feet: Men Interested by West Side New York's Auto Meetings... (1914, October). *Association Men*, 40(1), p. 40.

"I was not personally acquainted with Canada Blackie, but I did know intimately the members of his gang and all about the circumstances of the robbery for which he died in prison. Blackie was, at the time of the robbery, the pal of Canada Bob and Dublin Ned, well known yeggs. He had no connection with the men who actually blew the safe at Cobleskill, and I doubt if he knew them.

"What happened was this: Blackie and his two pals had Cobleskill as a mark and Blackie was sent up to look the job over. By mere coincidence he chose the very night which the other gang, without his knowledge, had chosen to commit the robbery. Naturally when the fight and killing happened, Blackie was in the neighborhood. The detectives picked him up and jobbed him. They sent him to prison and tried to send him to the chair under their customary attitude that any robber is guilty and it makes no difference of whose crime you manage to convict him.

"Whitey Sullivan and Goat Hinch went to the chair. Big Ed Kelly (Boston Eddie), is still serving his life sentence. Blackie, who had no more to do with the actual robbery than I, received what amounted to a term in prison with a death sentence at the end. Perhaps it will be urged he intended to rob the bank later and that intent is as bad as the deed."[36]

". . .intent is as bad as the deed." Words most certainly worthy of rumination as one pieces together the story, the fact, the life—the tragedy—of John E. Murphy, alias Jack, alias John Hamilton, alias Canada Blackie.

Remember: Do Good. Make Good.

---

[36] The illustration at right accompanied the article, which we believe may be based on one of Blackie's mugshots due to the cropped hair.

John E. Murphy
"Canada Blackie"
HONORARY HEATHEN

Do Good. Make Good.

www.ingramcontent.com/pod-product-compliance
Lightning Source LLC
Chambersburg PA
CBHW022054020426
42335CB00012B/688